TAPPING
INTO
WEALTH

TAPPING

INTO

WEALTH

How Emotional Freedom Techniques (EFT)
Can Help You Clear the Path
to Making More Money

MARGARET M. LYNCH

with Daylle Deanna Schwartz

JEREMY P. TARCHER/PENGUIN · A MEMBER OF PENGUIN GROUP (USA) · NEW YORK

TARCHER/PENGUIN
Published by the Penguin Group
Penguin Group (USA) LLC
375 Hudson Street
New York, New York 10014

USA · Canada · UK · Ireland · Australia
New Zealand · India · South Africa · China

penguin.com
A Penguin Random House Company

First trade paperback edition 2014
Copyright © 2013 by Margaret M. Lynch and Daylle Deanna Schwartz, M.S.

Most Tarcher/Penguin books are available at special quantity discounts for bulk purchase for sales promotions, premiums, fund-raising, and educational needs. Special books or book excerpts also can be created to fit specific needs. For details, write: Special.Markets@us.penguingroup.com.

The Library of Congress has catalogued the hardcover edition as follows:

Lynch, Margaret M.
Tapping into wealth: how Emotional Freedom Techniques (EFT) can help you clear the path to making more money/Margaret M. Lynch, Daylle Deanna Schwartz; (Foreword by) Nick Ortner.
p.   cm.
ISBN 978-0-399-16409-5
1. Finance, Personal—Psychological aspects.   2. Money—Psychological aspects.   3. Wealth—Psychological aspects.   I. Schwartz, Daylle Deanna.   II. Title.
HG179.L957   2013   2013028964
332.024'01019—dc23

ISBN 978-0-399-16882-6 (paperback)

Printed in the United States of America

Book design by Meighan Cavanaugh

CONTENTS

FOREWORD

In 2004, burdened by debt, tired of the roller-coaster ride of boom periods and bust periods, and unsatisfied with my daily work, I found myself looking for another answer. I knew that what I had been doing simply wasn't working, and it wasn't for lack of effort. I read the self-help books, I studied the financial courses, I strived to improve myself and my financial reality, but nothing seemed to "click."

It wasn't until I discovered EFT Tapping that everything changed for me. It was at that moment that I began to realize that what I had always thought was an "outer game"—working harder, getting lucky breaks, the economy—was really much more of an "inner game," as were my perceptions, decisions, belief systems, traumas, and more.

That awareness is a fantastic first step toward changing, but the question then remains, "How do I actually change? I know I've got some bad patterns, belief systems, and traumas, but what do I do about it?" This is where Tapping comes to the rescue, in extraordinary ways.

When I began Tapping in 2004, it helped me to clear out that old junk and create a new reality for myself. The documentary film about EFT—*The Tapping Solution*, now also a *New York Times*–bestselling book—which I set off to make in 2007, was a project inspired by a new way of being, a new reality, that said all things are possible, that I could make my dreams come true, and that I not only could provide incredible value and contributions to the world but could also be financially rewarded for them.

After I began Tapping to change my financial reality, the last six years of my life have been simply extraordinary. And I credit the success to the time I spent taking a close hard look at my financial beliefs and using Tapping to change them. This simple, scientifically validated process has made all the difference in my life, and it can do the same for you.

So I can guarantee you that there is no more powerful tool in the world to actualize change than Tapping. But there are times when the tool isn't enough, when you need the guidance, care, and nurturing of a powerful mentor who can pinpoint exactly where you need to go, what you need to explore, in order to get the fastest results possible.

And this is where my friend Margaret Lynch and this amazing book come in. Sure, you can learn the Tapping basics and use the process on your own. But it's likely to take longer, be more difficult, and generate results that are less powerful than what you will achieve with the laser-focused guidance of an expert like Margaret Lynch.

I met Margaret in 2008, at the dawn of both of our EFT "careers." Her bright smile and engaging personality instantly attracted me to her, and after spending time with her, I quickly learned that not only did Margaret exude success and confidence but she also had a deep understanding of money, finances, goal-setting, and all the key elements to creating lasting success.

I've watched Margaret during the past several years as she's continued to innovate on EFT, bringing a new and profound sense of clarity and enthusiasm, as well as impressive results, to this work. And with this book, she's taken all of that to the next level.

You hold in your hands the opportunity to be personally mentored by one of the smartest ladies I know. (She's coached me personally one-on-one on many occasions.) Her insights and her understanding of the material are unparalleled and can help you to quickly and efficiently change your financial reality.

So sit back, relax, get comfy, start Tapping, and begin the journey to finally unleashing your creative potential, following your dreams and passions, and creating a life of success and abundance!

—Nick Ortner, author of the *New York Times* bestseller *The Tapping Solution*

TAPPING INTO WEALTH

INTRODUCTION

*W*hy don't I have more money? I hear that over and over from people who are frustrated about feeling stuck in an income bracket, despite their strong desire and best efforts to have a lot more. Many work harder, yet don't reap the rewards of it. Others use the popular New Age idea of the Law of Attraction to create more wealth by consciously focusing their thoughts on it (more on this in chapter 1), but wonder why this doesn't end up working for them. Most feel frustrated, disappointed, and down on themselves for their inability to generate a larger income. Then the blame and excuses begin:

- "What's wrong with me that I can't make more money?"
- "What have I done to deserve this?"
- "I don't know how to make more money!"
- Etc., etc.

These negative messages and emotions reinforce what you *don't* want. It's time to change the dynamics between you and money! I wrote this book to help you overcome the main factors that block financial freedom by using powerful techniques. The power to change your money situation is in your hands, or more specifically, in your mind. It doesn't matter what's in your bank account or what your current income is. If you're willing to explore how past experiences create your current view of money, and release them, you can open the door to more money than you can imagine having. I personally built my current career using the strategies in this book. You can too! Once you understand what I teach you, the power to take charge of and *greatly* increase how much wealth you create and amass will be yours. I want you to be rich!

Unlike many well-known coaches using mind/body approaches, I come from a science and business background. I earned a bachelor of science in chemical engineering from Worcester Polytechnic Institute in Massachusetts and approach mind/body techniques with the practical mind-set of an engineer. After eighteen-plus years of management and executive sales experience at Fortune 500 companies, I decided to change my career path to become a success coach and had to deal with my own blocks against money and wealth.

My engineering background drew me to the new science of energy medicine, and I became a certified EFT (Emotional Freedom Techniques) Practitioner. EFT, which is also known as Tapping (more on this in chapter 2), requires using fingertips to tap on a specific series of acupuncture points while emotionally tuning in to limiting beliefs or negative experiences, and expressing feelings about them as you tap on these points. This mind/body technique lets you access your subconscious mind and physically release blocks. I started using EFT for myself and experienced major shifts in my attitudes, actions, and confidence.

When I began my business, New England Success Coaching, I had great expectations of success, especially because I was armed with this powerful technique. But as the months went by, I experienced fear, frustration, shame, and sadness about never quite making enough. I operated in survival mode—trying to make enough to pay my bills and survive, genuinely surprised at how difficult it was to earn a good living. Many smart, hardworking, well-intentioned individuals came to me for help. They were also stressed over their money situations—struggling simultaneously to make ends meet, enjoy life, and expand their business, talents, and lifestyle. They wanted to work with me on their confidence or public speaking and eliminate their stress, anxiety, or upsetting memories from the past. I observed how well they hid their private financial hell that in many cases was the source of their constant fear, pressure, and insecurity.

Many of these people were open-minded and had done lots of personal development work, but were still limited by money in their personal lives and businesses. This kept them stressed, stuck in fear, and held them back from enjoying life and making more of an effort to use their unique gifts and talents. The limitations in their wealth picture rippled out into all aspects of their lives, affecting their health, family, and career. It became clear that the common denominator in all my clients was struggle and limitation related to money, which meant that specific blocks to money were playing a significant role.

These blocks and limiting beliefs about money completely dictated their entire wealth picture—income, savings, the goals they set, and even how much debt they had. Many of these people were some of the greatest, most passionate, and talented people I'd ever met, which contributed to how much it bothered me. It just seemed wrong and unfair that such smart, positive, and willing people would struggle so much with money. It also hit very close to home, as I was experiencing similar struggles in my new business.

This frustration drove me to go deeper and figure out how to uncover and release blocks very specific to money and wealth. It pushed me to delve into my own internal blocks and into every teaching I could find about the subject. I discovered that at the core of limiting beliefs, struggles, and self-sabotage in relation to money are negative vows made unconsciously around money and wealth. Most originated long ago, usually in childhood, and have long since been forgotten on a conscious level. I studied patterns that I observed of how people handled their money and their attitudes to having money in general, and discovered how easy it is to recognize money blocks once you know where to look.

Tapping, combined with my research that specifically focused on money and wealth, made the clearing of money blocks a phenomenal success for me and for my clients. "Aha" moments gave people insight as they looked back at their lives and finally understood why they made mistakes related to money and success. This understanding allowed them to clear their specific blocks and limiting attitudes toward money so they could manifest more money and success with true freedom of choice. From that enlightenment, I created programs packed with tools to clear every block that limits and sabotages wealth. And it worked! Within a few years I rose to the top of my profession as a leading worldwide expert in EFT/Tapping for money.

In today's economic climate, a mind/body approach to money is more essential than ever! As you look at the world, you've seen the financial systems across the globe break down. Like old buildings, their structures are collapsing and need to be rebuilt, since most are based on a foundation of rules, beliefs, and ways of operating that are outdated, rarely questioned, and in many cases corrupt. And here's the real kicker: you reflect them. Imagine that you have an inner financial system like a city of old structures. Until now, your entire personal financial picture was built on these structures—a foundation of rules, beliefs, and ways of operating that are outdated, and often corrupted by shame, self-doubt, fear, and other negative emotions.

These inner tenets are as solid, rigid, and real as steel girders and cement foundations. Like a city of old buildings, they must be deconstructed to build a new wealth reality that supports your real life purpose. You can do it! While some doors close, huge new doors of opportunities are opening when you're ready to step through. I stepped through one when I left corporate America and became free of the zombie-job and fear of layoffs. But in order to succeed, I needed to do two key things:

- Deconstruct my inner financial buildings and upgrade my money operating systems
- Take a huge step up in my personal power, to increase enthusiasm, energy, brilliance, action, charisma, and choice

How huge is the step up you're willing to take to make more money? It will have to match the size of your goals for your mission and wealth. When I first started my business, I had an outrageous vision, so my steps had to be big and bold—and they were, once I got rid of the weight of my resistance to success. A key question to ask yourself is, "Have I reached my tipping point of pain yet, or does my life path still seem okay?" Are you frustrated about your financial situation or closer to outrage? Or are you just plain sick of it? If you have any or all of these emotions, or are just at a point where you're ready to have more money, read on! I'm thrilled to be able to help you open your own doors to increased wealth.

Throughout the book, I explain how to recognize where your blocks come from. First, I'll introduce you to the mind/body connection to money and how it affects your finances. I'll explain what Tapping is and how you can do it on your own. Then I'll present experiential exercises you can do that will help reveal your real beliefs and emotions about money and why you need to get serious about having a lot more. We'll examine hidden fears about the downsides of having a lot of money and how you might sabotage your ability to increase wealth by overspending, making bad investments, not managing bill payments, and the like. I'll also include guidance for resetting your wealth set point by shifting your subconscious beliefs about the limit of how much money you should have, which keeps you stuck. By the end of the book, you'll know why you don't have more money, and how you can shift that. Then you'll be ready to take the real steps to change.

I've helped thousands of people identify their resistance to getting lots of money, and use Tapping to clear blocks. Now I want to help *you* answer the question "Why don't I have more money?" so you can find and clear your own blocks and make a lot more money! Most chapters have specific exercises to help you get clarity about each lesson, as well as sample scripts to guide you as you use Tapping to clear blocks. I want to help you step out of what might seem a hopeless financial hell and open the door to a new wealth reality. You can do it! Let the following chapters guide you.

Each chapter also has a video with additional tips, excercises, and Tapping to supercharge your progress. You can find the video by following the QR Code or URL provided at the end of each chapter.

1

THE MIND/BODY
MONEY CONNECTION

The mind/body connection has gotten lots of exposure in the last decade, most commonly related to health. Dr. John Sarno's best-selling books, including *Mind Over Back Pain*, and Louise L. Hay's book *You Can Heal Your Life* discuss a mind/body connection between negative emotions and illness and how to use it to ease or let go of health problems. I use the same principles for increasing wealth.

If you want to greatly increase your wealth, it's important to recognize that money has a mind/body component. You can harness this to take control of and increase how much you have. But using it isn't as effortless as it may sound. It requires you to look within for answers, and face old memories or limiting beliefs that could be painful. Finding your personal mind/body connection to money can be the hardest part of this journey, but when you do find it, the rewards can reflect enormously in your bank account.

Isn't Using the Law of Attraction Enough?

When Oprah featured people from the DVD for *The Secret* on her show, people rushed to manifest their desires, using what was explained about the Law of Attraction. But they found it wasn't nearly as easy as it was portrayed on the show. Some of the most important factors for using the Law of Attraction properly weren't discussed.

The Law of Attraction works on the basic principle that you'll literally draw to you—attract, create, and receive—more of whatever you consciously focus on with intent. So the idea of using the Law of Attraction means you can purposely put your attention on what you'd like to have, or have more of, and it will show up. There are two major challenges with that. The first is that a majority of people mainly use their conscious thoughts as the key to receiving their desires, or they just visualize what they want and ignore the rest of their vibes. But you're way more than just those thoughts! Your vibration—your strongest emotions—about a desire is the sum of your positive and negative feelings about it.

In addition, your emotions, programmed limitations related to getting what you deserve or are capable of earning, and expectations about your desire that took root from childhood on also strongly affect what you get. That's why understanding the mind/body connection is so critical. For example, you can visualize having a million dollars every day. But your subconscious may believe things like:

- "That's a hundred percent impossible."
- "It's wrong to want so much money."
- "No one in my family ever got a lot although they worked very hard."

The Law of Attraction picks up on the vibes behind those thoughts, even if you don't consciously acknowledge having them. Those kinds of beliefs can turn your overall vibe about your vision into one of disempowerment, disbelief, and guilt. If you actually create a goal to earn a million dollars, it would likely trigger negative emotions like anxiety or fear of failure. This mind/body reaction is also known as the "stress response" and is directly connected to money.

All of this changes the entire chain reaction of how you interact with everyone and everything. This overall vibe keeps you from being open to inspiration and creative ideas that lead to creating wealth. It's hard to take enthusiastic action toward earning a large amount of money if your negative beliefs and emotions fight your desire. Without a clear positive vibration about the money you want, you won't be inspired to share your vision with others who might give you ideas, invest in your visions, or support you. According to medical literature, the stress response is a physiological state in which your actual ability to think creatively and expansively is greatly reduced because your brain is focused on being in survival mode, which I'll talk about more in chapter 4.

For the Law of Attraction to work in your favor, you need to be passionately positive enough to generate a positive vibration about money, visualize your dreams becoming real, and believe that big goals can be achieved. How can you do that if you're only focused on paying bills and having just enough to get by? How can you feel good about your big goals if they seem almost impossible? At that point, the emotions that money triggers are too powerful at the wrong end of the spectrum for manifesting. Negative emotions, often unconscious, block your ability to attract a positive outcome.

You can't just think about what you desire to manifest it. Your entire vibe must match your desire. If you have doubt, fear, feelings of not deserving, and so on about what you say you want, you probably won't get it. Instead, you'll attract people and situations that align with those feelings and reinforce the idea that you don't deserve it or that it's impossible. It's important to recognize that the Law of Attraction picks up on both conscious thoughts and those below the tip of your thinking and visualizing, where there's a huge iceberg of resistance to getting what you say you desire.

A second challenge for using the Law of Attraction to increase wealth is that you must be specific about what you want. When asked what they'd like to manifest most, a majority of people say, "More money!" If you're reading this book, you probably agree. But the strange thing is that most people who try to use the Law of Attraction, or who simply make an effort to better their lives with personal development work, are unwilling to get clear about their specific money desire. They avoid stating specific money and wealth goals with actual dollar signs next to them, in favor of the much more fun "winning the hundred-million-dollar lottery" dreams or just wanting "more," which doesn't make the desire clear.

Why the lack of definite goals? With all the negative associations you may have related to money and wealth, focusing directly on a precise amount will start to create stress, anxiety, guilt, fear of failure, and often negative self-talk. It can be painful, so avoiding thoughts of specific money goals can become an unconscious reflex to keep from triggering negative feelings. Yet those feelings are there. That's why so many people get frustrated when they find that the Law of Attraction doesn't attract more money for them. If all it took to get what you want were to desire it, we'd all have financial security. While you may repeat affirmations, set intentions, and do all the other work recommended by leading experts, you won't attract the level of money you have the potential to get until you:

- Put all your focus on a specific money goal.
- Resolve and clear old blocks, traumas, etc.—your resistance to getting what you say you want.

Understanding Blocks/Resistance

If you've read about the Law of Attraction, you know the importance of clearing resistance in order to use it to your advantage. It may sound simple—just clear the resistance and you'll get what you want—but most people don't know where to begin. Resistance to achieving goals is created by all the blocks you've accumulated since childhood. They come in many sizes and flavors. Even though you may consciously feel you want something badly, just below the surface there's a collection of beliefs, emotions, and programming that directly refuse it.

Everyone has his or her own individual blocks. Each bad memory, everything that scares you, all the doubts that became ingrained as you experienced disappointment, deceit, being let down by someone you trusted, all the unworthiness you felt when someone criticized you, failing at an endeavor you believed in, or not doing well in school—all the negative experiences, beliefs, and observations—add up to resistance to having more money. For example, you may say you'd love to be rich, but if your subconscious absolutely refuses to be rich or even try, it won't happen. This part of your subconscious is an accumulation of all of your programmed beliefs and emotions related to money that have become your absolute truth. It's not based on logic or reason.

Unfortunately, a large part of how you operate stems from your subconscious mind. You're usually not aware of these negative blocks, but they strongly influence your behavior. This subconscious resistance may motivate you to make excuses for not applying for a better job, to overspend, to invest in something risky, to procrastinate doing things that could improve your financial picture, and to behave in a million other ways that might be responsible for your not having the level of wealth you'd like. If you become aware of your blocks, it can be hard to figure out how to clear them. Even when life takes a very positive turn, negative blocks have a much more powerful effect on how you behave and can change your circumstances quickly.

A study at Vanderbilt University found that pain has a stronger effect on you than pleasure has. Other studies show that negative emotions often have much stronger sticking power and longevity than positive ones, which tend to dissipate more easily. Fear, doubt, guilt, and the like lock into your subconscious. Good feelings from positives may dissolve soon after your situation changes. Negative emotions linger as reminders of what to avoid later on. You may feel excited if a friend shares his plan to start a business and wants you to join him. You go home eager to take the plunge. This is your chance to leave a job that's going nowhere, and do something you've dreamed of doing! But by morning, old memories of your dad failing when he tried to start a business, leaving your family struggling to pay bills, can stop you from doing it. Even if your new opportunity is much better than the business your dad had and chances of the business succeeding are good, the fire you felt initially will probably be doused by negative memories.

Or, you feel revved up when given a big pep talk about how talented you are and why you should pursue opportunities to use your gifts for more rewarding work. That praise feels great and you can't wait to start. It's what you always wanted to do. But those feelings can be overshadowed quickly by subconscious memories of being told you'd never amount to anything and shouldn't bother pursuing your dreams. Doubts and fear of failure can wipe out all those positive feelings, no matter how badly you want to run with all the joy you felt. So you just wait for opportunities to come to you instead of going after a lucrative career. Then you wonder if you'll ever have a more satisfying career.

Since most people have had negative experiences related to money, whether at home as a child or in adulthood, money is probably the hardest thing to manifest with the Law of Attraction. The more emotional baggage you have in relation to money, the more likely you can't get or keep the amount you'd like to have, no matter what you do.

So the answer to "Why don't I have more money?" lies in your subconscious.

Neuroscience says that only about 15 percent of your mind is conscious. Your subconscious is 85 percent of your mind and holds all your habits, beliefs, and memories. Bruce Lipton, Ph.D., author of *The Biology of Belief*, describes it this way: "The subconscious mind is running programs that are a million times more powerful than the processing abilities of the conscious mind." Why don't you have more money? Your conscious, positive thoughts about making more money compete with the programming contained in your much more powerful subconscious, which resists your desires. This makes it tricky to be both aware of and get rid of blocks that interfere with your efforts and desire to have more.

This inner conflict between what people say or think they want and their blocks is what leaves them scratching their heads about why they behave as they do. It makes them wonder why they procrastinate on the very actions that would make them more money, or totally avoid setting goals. Or, they puzzle over why the thought of asking for a raise or increasing their fees or getting paid for talent they give away fills them with fear and anxiety. These inner blocks are the culprits when brilliant financial experts like CPAs make disastrous choices in their personal finances or when someone rises in success and income only to lose everything.

Jen came to me after hearing me speak and identified herself as a joke of an accountant. She'd done well in school, and her clients thought she was smart about money. Yet she struggled with her own finances and was frustrated and puzzled about why. During my talk, she thought about how her mother always used to say that women weren't supposed to be smart about money, and men were intimidated by women who were. It was ironic that she became an accountant, but she realized that in her personal life, she had become the helpless female that her mother had taught her to be. It was a pivotal moment for her, and she was able to clear the block and greatly improve her finances.

You may set a very clear intention for what you want and wonder why it's not working. Chances are, subconscious blocks cancel it out. They lead you to set the bar low and not ask for as much as you could, and should. It can get frustrating when you sabotage your money intention and don't know why. Subconscious emotions hijack your freedom of choice and you become bound by invisible chains. When it comes to money, you're up against very specific blocks. As you do the exercises in later chapters, you'll begin to recognize them. You deserve the freedom to choose what to do and have in your life! I'll help you achieve that in your financial picture.

Throughout the book I'll explain the different kinds of blocks people have so you can identify your own. They can be hard to find, especially if they're painful, but finding them helps you understand why you don't have more money. Your mind may try to keep your blocks hidden to protect you. It's your job to uncover them. Once you do, you can start lowering your resistance by clearing the blocks, one by one. Releasing them is truly the key to your freedom and wealth!

The Secret Story and Power of Your Subconscious Mind: Get a deeper understanding of how your subconscious mind operates, why people really self-sabotage, and how shifting this part of your mind results in a quantum leap forward.
www.TappingIntoWealth.com/Video1

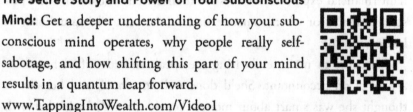

2

THE BASICS OF TAPPING

I want you to stop asking "Why don't I have more money?" and do something to change your financial situation. In the Introduction, I referred to the use of Tapping to clear blocks that keep you from having more money. Once you learn how to do it—it's very simple—and recognize blocks that create resistance to having more money, your power to clear resistance will be strong. If you've never heard of Tapping, get ready for something that may seem weird and outside the box. Tapping is a mind-set technique used to overcome limiting beliefs, fears, self-esteem issues, and even things like post-traumatic stress disorder and anxiety.

Tapping is one of the most powerful and effective mind/body techniques for clearing emotional blocks that keep you from achieving what you want. While the idea of it may seem unpromising, or even ridiculous, when I first explain it, you'll change your mind quickly when you see results. And there's science behind it, with more than forty clinical trials attesting to the efficacy of Tapping for PTSD, anxiety, and even phobias! Because it lets you access your subconscious mind, Tapping can clear blocks that subconsciously hold you back from what you want, including having more money. It gives you freedom to get more by dissolving resistance that keeps the Law of Attraction from working for you at full capacity. The biggest proof is found in trying it!

Why Tap?

Tapping is a technique used to heal emotions. It's also known as EFT (Emotional Freedom Techniques), which was brought to people's attention throughout the 1980s and 1990s by Gary Craig. Tapping is also called TFT, based on the original technique developed by Roger Callahan. It was initially created to treat phobias and severe post-traumatic stress disorder because you can effectively turn off some of the memories with Tapping. It's being used successfully to help veterans and victims of mass genocide ease their PTSD. When you use Tapping, it frees you from negative emotions tied to limiting beliefs, fears, and old memories that unconsciously block your desires. Once you clear these with Tapping, the blocks are released and you have the emotional freedom to make good things happen.

Tapping has been reported as successful in many thousands of cases for a wide range of issues. It often gets results for problems and situations that nothing else does. My specialty is using Tapping for success-focused people who want to break free of specific blocks that prevent them from growing their business, stepping into their mission, and amassing more money. Many people are surprised that I use Tapping with business professionals and entrepreneurs. But this technique is needed for these areas because people do not act logically when it comes to their money. You can get incredibly emotional, even if you're not aware of it.

Tapping was developed around the principles of acupuncture, which has been used to clear energy blocks and heal health issues for thousands of years in Chinese medicine. It was then found that if you use acupressure in the form of tapping lightly with your fingertips on acupuncture points, you can make a shift in unconscious beliefs and negative emotions that block you from getting what you want. Medical doctors now recognize that our bodies have a kind of electrical system that flows through it. In Eastern philosophy, this is called the "meridian system," and the energy is called "chi." If the chi flows as it should along the meridian, it keeps your body in a natural state of well-being. Using acupuncture stimulates points along the meridians that help clear energy blocks and get chi flowing in ways that help restore your well-being. The popularity of acupuncture continues to increase because of this.

In Western medicine, this electrical system has been associated with the fight-or-flight autonomic system, the sympathetic nervous system in the body. When you start Tapping on specific acupuncture points, you can actually flip a switch—an electrical circuit disconnect—and turn off reaction to something you're thinking about, which could be a memory, something that scares you, your bills, or something that makes you angry or sad. It can also flip the switch related to feelings about having to face your boss about a stressful issue or to deal with someone you dislike. Tapping disconnects the thought from the autonomic nervous reaction in the body, which means all the negative emotions dissipate and get calmer. At a physiological level, it calms the sympathetic nervous system responsible for the stress response and turns on the parasympathetic nervous system responsible for the relaxation response.

You have many emotions about all kinds of areas related to money. I even work with people who deal well with other people's money for a living—CPAs, financial planners, and other money experts. They help their clients manage their money effectively. But when it comes to their own finances, they become emotional, and all their limiting beliefs show up. Tapping is the best technique to quickly shift emotional states, limiting beliefs, and old memories and traumas that people have connected to their money and success.

IS TAPPING RIGHT FOR YOU?

If you've never tried Tapping, you may wonder if you should bother to use it, especially if you've never tried any alternative or energy treatments and don't believe it can work. My answer is always a big resounding *"Yes!"* You don't need to believe it can help. Just do it and see for yourself how well it works. I admit, Tapping looks strange. But it has been clinically proven effective multiple times and is used by some of the top people in the personal development and success fields, including Jack Canfield, Anthony "Tony" Robbins, and T. Harv Eker, because it's so effective for moving forward with goals.

Tapping has been endorsed by Deepak Chopra. Whoopi Goldberg used it to eliminate her fear of flying. Richard Branson has incorporated Tapping into the Virgin Atlantic "Flying Without Fear" program. Some reasons to learn Tapping are:

- Anyone can learn how to do it
- It doesn't take long to get the technique down
- You can do some Tapping in just a few minutes
- It's free to do, though some people find it helpful to work with a practitioner
- You can do it anytime, anywhere
- It can yield great results quickly

Throughout the book, I'll guide you through Tapping exercises to release blocks that keep you from making the kind of money you'd like. It may force you to look at things that aren't pleasant, but it will also help you let go of them so you can move forward into greater financial solvency.

THE TAPPING POINTS

It's easy to do Tapping! Express your feelings as you tap lightly on the acupuncture points explained below, using two fingers (or more) with either hand, or both hands. This is why Tapping is called "acupressure for the emotions." As long as you stimulate the points, it doesn't matter which hand or which side you tap on. While there are many more acupuncture points, I'll describe the ones most commonly used. If you watch different Tapping videos, you'll see people use a variety of points. They all work! If a point is uncomfortable to reach, like the one under your arm, skip it. You *can't* do Tapping wrong! If you follow my scripts and find yourself saying something that's not true for you, it's fine too. Nothing you say will hurt you.

Often Tapping begins with what's called "the setup." This is done to set up your energy to be most receptive to the rest of the Tapping rounds. For that, you tap on the center of the outside of either hand, called "the karate chop point," named for the part of the hand used to do a karate chop. You can use several fingers to make sure you hit the spot. As you tap, voice a negative feeling, emotion, or belief several times to keep you focused on it. What you say each time is related to what you said just before it. It usually follows a pattern such as: "Even though I feel [negative feeling], I still [positive statement]. For example, "Even though I feel really anxious about the bills right now, I still honor all my feelings." The point of this is to get you more in touch with emotions you need to release. Sometimes you won't need the setup and you can just start tapping and voicing what you're feeling. In the Tapping exercises throughout the book, sometimes I use a setup and sometimes I don't. As I said, there's no wrong way to do Tapping.

The points I typically use for Tapping are those commonly used by acupuncturists, but luckily we don't need any needles! Instead, we use Tapping to create a light electrical charge to literally shift what's happening in your body and nervous system. I use eight main points and begin at the eyebrow. You can check the diagram to make sure you have the right spots. These are the points in the order that I use them.

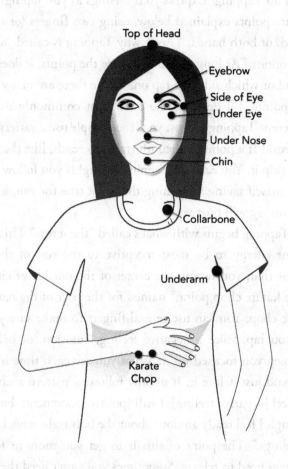

- **Eyebrow point:** on the inside of your eyebrow
- **Side of the eye point:** right on the edge of the bone on the side of the eye
- **Under the eye point:** in the center of the top edge of the bone under the eye
- **Under the nose:** between the nose and upper lip

- **Chin point**: in the cleft of your chin
- **Collarbone point**: find the U-shaped bone at the base of your neck and follow either side down at an angle to find a slight depression. That's where you tap.
- **Underarm point**: about four inches down from your armpit (where a bra band falls on women)
- **Top of the head point**: at the center of the head

Some people begin at the top of the head. It all works. These are the points I've found most helpful, but don't worry if you do it a bit differently.

HOW DO I KNOW WHAT TO SAY?

The fuel for effective Tapping is voicing words that connect to the negative emotions, limiting beliefs, and intensity of resistance you might feel, often subconsciously, when thinking about something you want to change. I'll guide you through getting in touch with these feelings in every chapter. Once you tune in to your resistance, you can start Tapping on these points and express your feelings. The more emotion you put behind your words, the better, since it's the emotions you need to release. So I'll encourage you to feel the words with every ounce of emotion you can muster. It's sometimes helpful to start by exaggerating emotions to seem bigger than what you think you might feel in order to trigger emotions you might be ignoring.

Most of the chapters include Tapping scripts. As you get more comfortable doing it, substitute feelings and other words that relate more to you and your situation. It's good to do one round with my words. If you're clearing something that causes a lot of negative emotions, do the round several times. Most scripts have both a negative and positive round. Once you feel your negative emotions subside about what you Tap on, move on to the positive round.

Throughout the book I'll tell you how to use Tapping to clear your biggest blocks to more wealth, personal power, and success in your life. It's a very powerful tool that can help you make effective changes in your finances and more. And you'll be able to feel that change happening very clearly.

How to Tap: A demonstration of how to do Tapping and where to find the Tapping points www.TappingIntoWealth.com/Video2

3

THE FIVE CATEGORIES
OF MONEY

P eople tend to lump all money issues together, but it's not as simple as that. I've identified five different categories of money—income, savings, debt, income and wealth goals, and toxic money. Every category represents a different aspect of how you deal with and manage your money and wealth. It's important to look at these categories individually, since each elicits its own set of feelings and beliefs, and when examined, reveals a whole set of programming that has been downloaded into you from childhood to the present. In this chapter, I present an overview of the five categories of money to help you identify how each plays a role in your life. I'll go into more details when they come up in later chapters.

Abundance and Prosperity versus Money

Before I discuss the five types of money, I want to point out the fact that I don't include the big buzzwords found in many books and workshops about manifesting more: "abundance" and "prosperity." That's because they're not specific types of money and won't help determine where your blocks are. Abundance and prosperity are very generalized concepts that are often used as euphemisms for money in the self-help and Law of Attraction movements. But these words aren't directly associated with the actual handling of cash, income, debt, paying bills, and so on. Most people actually don't feel blocks related to abundance and prosperity at all, since they're just concepts.

I believe we often use the terms "abundance" and "prosperity" to avoid doing exactly what I'm about to make you do in the next chapters—tune in to how you actually feel about money. We're taught to include all the non-money riches we have—good health, family and friends, love, joy—under the umbrella of abundance. It sounds good, and can make you feel better for the moment about not having more money to spend, save, pay off bills, or invest. But thinking in those terms can distract you from doing something constructive to change your financial situation.

There's nothing wrong with seeking the kind of abundance I just described. But sometimes that mind-set can make you feel guilty about wanting lots more cold cash and/or get you off the track for creating it. Seeking to increase abundance can seem like a more spiritual mind-set, while focusing on just getting more money can seem shallow. It can almost seem as if you don't appreciate all the blessings that encompass your abundance. So homing in on more money as a goal can trigger guilt. But you can't pay bills with abundance! Nor can you upgrade your lifestyle if you can't pay for it.

If you want a lot more money, you need to focus directly on increasing your dollar value. Of course you can also appreciate other kinds of abundance, as long as you focus on money when that's what you want. After all, you can build your determination to greatly improve your financial picture by both feeling gratitude about all your blessings *and* focusing on creating much more abundance in dollars and cents.

INCOME

The first category of money is income—your earned money. Income is the direct flow of money into your life that's received in exchange for your time and energy. It represents both survival and the level at which you value yourself: your energy, time, training, and experience. Thinking about your income can trigger and reveal programmed emotions around survival in society. It indicates how you were taught to view your ability to thrive or just survive, and what socioeconomic class you're in. Ask yourself:

- Am I just barely surviving, living hand to mouth?
- Is my family considered to be middle class but it feels like I never have enough for the things I want to improve my life?
- Do I bring in enough to make ends meet but always run out of money by the end of the month?

In addition to signifying where you stand between surviving and thriving, your income is also a metaphorical reflection of your belief about your personal and professional market value. While outside factors such as the marketplace rate for skill, experience, education, and the like will influence this value, the main factor lies in you and your life history. The key to your income level is your belief in your personal worth and the value of what you do or give. That explains in part why many people with no educational training rise to great success while just as many with every credential under the sun have a hard time asking for or going after what they're worth.

People argue that their company or job description sets their value. Yet many people in the same company are paid more than average because of their unique value. So if your belief in your value is low, subconsciously you'll always either keep your income low or work very hard for your money. You may blame people or circumstances for your economic situation, but that needs to stop if you want to increase your income. The reality is, the money you earn is a reflection of what you believe you deserve at a deep level, based on your programmed feelings and beliefs about how valuable you are. If you suddenly start to earn more than your inner-worth set point thinks you should, you'll subconsciously find a way to work harder, longer hours, sabotage it, or somehow sacrifice more to make it feel fair.

I worked with an executive salesperson named Diane who made great money but was chronically exhausted and confused about why she worked three times harder and longer than the other salespeople. Diane revealed that her father, who was her hero, often told her while growing up, "You've got to work hard and be perfect." He worked in corporate America his whole life and prided himself on working long hours. I asked Diane how much she felt she needed to work to deserve the big salary she earned. She answered, "About sixty hours a week," adding, "I feel that's fair."

Diane had a huge "aha" moment when she saw the conflict in that, but didn't know how to change this inner feeling of fairness related to the amount of time she worked. While she complained about being chronically tired and ill, her inner voice felt this was fair. I challenged her further, asking what if all her work to land a big new account could be leveraged to land a second large account with only 20 percent more effort—doubling her sales commissions without doubling the time expended. Would it feel fair to get paid more without really working more hours? She answered, "Absolutely not!"

We unraveled the fact that Diane created ways to drag out her work until it took sixty hours a week. Many subconscious actions made her job take longer, or she ignored the things she could do to seal deals faster. She made sure that the time she put in compensated for what she earned. She often suffered from exhaustion, was disorganized and confused, ran late, forgot things, questioned her ability, and asked for more validation than necessary. These factors helped drag out her work time. Recognizing this was life altering for Diane. She was able to challenge her old belief directly and begin to adopt a new belief, with the mantra "Work smarter, not harder." From this new belief, her brilliance, organizational skills, and actions aligned to create efficient, streamlined activities that allowed her to be a top-producing sales rep working thirty-five hours a week.

There will always be a give-and-take exchange that involves your belief in the value of your time, energy, intelligence, and level of education and training, and the amount of work that you need to put in to deserve to earn your income. As illustrated by Diane's situation, thinking about income triggers both the emotion around survival and a self-definition of your worth. Understanding the dynamics gives you power to change it.

SAVINGS

The second category of money—savings—is a totally different animal. You may earn plenty of income yet feel like you live one paycheck away from disaster if you have no savings. Accruing some provides a buffer against emergencies and increases security. It's hard to feel secure knowing an unexpected expense could arise and you have no cushion. Having savings helps you feel safe, secure, and calmer about your finances. Similar to thoughts about income, thinking about your savings, or lack thereof, triggers its own set of emotions, limiting beliefs, and past traumas surrounding money that relate to whether or not you feel safe in a broader sense than just day-to-day life.

Having savings also means you've gone beyond survival to the freedom to make choices based on what you find interesting, pleasurable, or exciting, instead of just limiting your expectations based on your income. When thinking about your lack of a savings safety net, you may find yourself experiencing a layer of anxiety barely covering profound sadness, and even a sense of loss. It tends to bring up memories or somehow connect emotionally to a great loss in your or your parents' lives that's still being grieved for or regretted.

Having little or no savings may echo a time when you lost something important or someone special, or you felt a loss of freedom on some level. It can even trigger emotions from times when you felt like you lost yourself. These past times of great loss may also be partially responsible for your lack of financial security because the lack of savings triggers the same feelings of loss, abandonment, or feeling totally unsupported. These are powerful negative emotions connected to something as practical as a savings account. While it's simple to create one by implementing a plan, it's unlikely to work if old emotional content is mixed up in your feelings about it.

Jessica came to my workshop full of cheery energy and the confidence of a successful salesperson, eager to work on her big income goals. But when we got to savings account goals, her whole energy shifted. I'd directed the group to think about how much money they currently have in their savings and write down any thoughts or feelings about it. Jessica immediately reported feeling consumed by tremendous anxiety and panic, with the thought, "It's not enough! What will happen to me if things get worse?" This thought woke her during the night because she had no savings at all.

After we did Tapping to reduce the anxiety and panic, I asked what else she felt about the zero savings balance. Tears flowed as Jessica revealed that nine years before, she had a partner who developed cancer when they were about to break up. Out of compassion and loyalty, she stayed and cared for him for two years instead of implementing her plan to move to New York and further her career. She even quit her job when the care got intense. He ran out of money and she drained her savings to help him, not able to desert a dying man she'd once loved.

Jessica was exhausted and drained physically, emotionally, and financially. While she grieved his passing, she couldn't let go of the anger and blame she felt toward this man about the toll it took on her life and finances. All the feelings of personal loss, grief, impossible choices, and anger were there whenever she thought about her lack of savings. So for nine years she avoided thinking about it, looking at it, or making a plan to change it, while frittering away big commission checks. Avoiding the negative emotions made her ignore planning for a savings account.

After a few rounds of Tapping to clear old feelings, Jessica felt ready to focus on putting money away. A few days later, she reported that she'd met with an adviser at her bank to set up an automatic deposit plan to move money from her paychecks into a savings account—part of her new one-year savings goal. She was amazed at how much lighter she felt in general and how excited she was to watch her savings account grow. While she felt a bit silly about it, she went online several times a day just to look at the balance, since it made her feel so happy and empowered.

Many people who work with emotions and beliefs around their lack of savings end up processing great grief and sadness from past events that feel directly connected to their finances, like Jessica's did. You may also create a self-definition based on what your lack of savings means about who you are: someone with no security, no freedom, and no support. This can be particularly painful if you're the head of a household and feel responsible for your family. Not having the security that a savings account brings can make you feel like a failure to them. Thinking about it can trigger feelings about letting down your family, which adds an intensely negative layer of emotion onto whether or not you take action to start saving money.

DEBT

The third category of money is debt, which by far has the most damaging emotional power of all the types of money. For most people with accumulated debt, thinking about it directly can bring up some of the darkest emotions one can experience. People typically report feeling deep and overwhelming shame, embarrassment, failure, anxiety, fear, and sadness. Debt can be an energetic manifestation of subconscious old memories of shame and feeling that you're not good enough to be financially solvent.

Being in debt can trigger an inner emotional response that's similar to the one that comes from not having any savings. But being in debt goes much deeper. Throughout the day, your mind may turn to thoughts of debt, either very consciously or barely realizing you were thinking about what you owe. It can be subtly pervasive. But strong negative emotions get triggered each time it brushes your thoughts. It's also common to wake during the night feeling overwhelmed by racing thoughts about the awful things that could happen from being in debt. Money debt can also strongly trigger negative self-talk and beliefs such as "I'm a failure" and "I don't deserve to be happy."

Because debt carries so much negative emotional baggage, it's also the type of money that people most often avoid dealing with directly. In our society, it's universally accepted that talking about your debt is tantamount to admitting you're a financial failure. Plus, it's embarrassing. So a majority of people who do Law of Attraction work, using positive thinking and focusing on abundance, rarely consider how the energy, emotions, or beliefs about their debt impact their positive work.

On a positive note, if you have debt, it means that a lending institution or person gave you credit by lending you money. If you want to help the Law of Attraction work on your behalf, create positive thoughts about being in debt. Think about how someone loaned you money and you're doing your best to repay it. Raise your positive vibration with an enthusiastic version of, "*Yes,* I am a person of integrity, and excellent when it comes credit!" Not all debt is bad. There may be times that you want or need a loan, and that's okay if you frame it in a positive way. People borrow money for good reasons all the time and repay it in ways that improve their credit rating.

But, similar to how thinking about your income triggers anxiety, the thought of owing money more often makes you feel bad, even if it's not bad. These intense emotions and beliefs can contribute to disastrous financial situations. Dealing with the emotions, limiting beliefs, and your personal definition of debt can be one of the most powerful transformational elements in your life and finances.

Jeff came to work with me months after shutting down the restaurant that had been his dream. He was having trouble interviewing for a job and believed it was rooted in his loss of confidence. When I asked about his biggest obstacle, he admitted that debt from his failed business made him feel like a loser. After he bought it, he quickly realized he'd been misled by the seller about what he'd need to invest for renovations and how much revenue he could generate. Even when he realized the truth, he stayed confident about being able to turn a profit with his wife and father-in-law's support and hard work.

Jeff got emotional sharing his story about their five years of working long, exhausting hours and slowly draining their savings and retirement accounts to keep the restaurant afloat. Besides losing the business and their money, he had debt. It overwhelmed him with shame, sadness, grief, and lots of guilt. Every thought of it reminded Jeff of everything his wife and elderly father-in-law sacrificed for him and how he'd lost it all. He believed he'd ruined their lives and constantly beat himself up about how stupid he was for being tricked by the dishonest seller. I heard "I should have known better!" often.

Jeff pointed to himself as a terrible, unforgivable, naive, and clueless businessman. He couldn't imagine how he could ever exude confidence again. As we used Tapping to clear this intense negative emotion and self-talk about past mistakes, Jeff was finally able to see how his experience made him more savvy and enlightened as a business consultant. Instead of being ashamed of his story, he started telling it during interviews to reveal how passionate he was about being a consultant. Once he let go of his need to wallow in guilt and other emotions from losing his restaurant, he turned his life around, which led directly to repaying his debts quickly.

INCOME AND WEALTH GOALS

The fourth category of money relates to goals for income and increased wealth. I call this a type of money because when you set a goal for your income, it reveals a whole new set of emotions, limiting beliefs, and fears. The reality is, no matter how high or low your current income is, it matches your inner belief about the value of your time and energy. When you try to go beyond that to increase your income with a goal in mind, you'll feel resistance.

You can have a good level of success and still be held back by your feelings about setting goals for making more money. For example, Stephanie was an in-demand web designer. She came to my workshop to clear her blocks to bigger success. She'd been in business for four years but earned the same amount every year and wanted to increase that. Each participant had to create an income goal for their business in advance, based on how much money they desired to get from it. I made it clear that it shouldn't be based on what they thought their business could generate. Stephanie's income goal was only $10,000 a year more than her current income and way below what she needed to pay bills and enjoy her life fully.

She confessed that she originally wrote a huge income goal but looking at it made her feel anxious, uncomfortable, even nauseous. So she made it smaller many times until her number was very close to her current income, which felt more comfortable. When I asked for her specific negative thoughts about writing the higher number, she had a whole list. On top was, "It's impossible," followed by "I have no idea how to get there." These two negative beliefs about a huge goal felt extremely strong. It translated into: "If I really set that goal, I'd very likely fail."

Subconsciously, Stephanie believed that committing to a goal that seemed impossible would set her up for painful failure, disappointment, and lots of embarrassment. And the majority of the people in the room felt it too! After we did some Tapping to reduce the intensity of those two strong beliefs, a third one came up that triggered sadness: "I'll probably work so hard that I'll never see my family." This big goal represented Stephanie's fears of failure and of being a bad mother. Yet if she wanted to be more successful, she had to pursue the big goal. She left with clarity about how to use Tapping to dispel limiting beliefs so her big goal could spark ideas and excitement to go for it. She e-mailed a week later that she revised her goal again—this time to increase it.

Setting an income goal is the first step to changing your financial picture. There's no success book on the planet that doesn't talk about the virtues of setting goals. Yet most people avoid them because the emotions and limiting beliefs start once you push the envelope. If you're self-employed or own your own business, not taking this step costs you the most money. If you're an employee, you may argue that it's useless to set an income goal since you have no control over it. The truth is, there's an infinite number of ways your income could double, triple, or quadruple. It happens all the time and can happen to you—*if* you allow it.

TOXIC MONEY

I call the fifth category "toxic money." You may not have any in your life, but when you do, it can be the most disempowering type of energetic money block there is. Toxic money is essential cash you need to survive but that comes with a negative emotional price or battle, usually from a source you'd love to be rid of but depend on for survival. For example, if you're owed alimony you desperately need, the party paying may be angry and resentful about paying it, forcing you to battle in the victim role. It creates an energy of having to prove you need the money to survive or having to counter arguments that you don't need it.

Being dependent on that kind of money creates an association between money and anger, guilt, and the need to battle. Your every feeling about money may go to negative places because of it. Battles over an inheritance also fall into this category. When someone feels that he or she has a right to receive one, and it's withheld in a way that feels unjust—being bullied or made to feel like a victim, for example—the money becomes toxic. It can make you eventually look back and say, "Since that day I've never been able to earn money." It's truly toxic if it keeps you feeling helpless, unable to control what you feel is rightfully yours. In addition, self-loathing can develop from knowing you need that money and are unable to take care of yourself without it.

Being in an unhealthy relationship with someone you rely on to take care of you financially also creates toxic money. If you feel trapped—needing their money to survive or maintain a lifestyle you're used to—negative emotions build. Every thought about being supported and having to stay in the relationship carries extreme loathing, anger, shame, and disgust. Your relationship may suffer from all the resentment that builds around needing to be taken care of and feeling like you can't take care of yourself.

Mark came to me after leaving a lucrative job. He spent his time on recreational activities, not actively seeking work, and mostly talked about the battle over his inheritance. Two years earlier, his father passed away, leaving him and his siblings enough money to ensure that Mark wouldn't have to work again, even with his daughter entering college. But one of his siblings, an attorney, contested the will, claiming Mark was illegitimate and should be completely cut out of the will and family. He had the money and know-how to keep the court battle going.

Mark was consumed with shock, anger, and hurt at the accusations and how he was being robbed. He still had unresolved grief from losing his father and the gift his father intended for him. The unfairness of his brother's actions and the very personal way in which he was betrayed, in the attempt to kick him out of the family in shame, outraged him. He was almost broke, about to lose his home, and unable to afford his daughter's college tuition. He explained that he didn't look for a job because when he had his good one, his brother used that as a reason for why Mark didn't need or deserve his inheritance.

So he stopped working. His increasingly dire situation motivated his other siblings to advocate for him out of compassion. The more broken, pathetic, and poor he looked, the closer he got not only to his inheritance, but also to triumphing over his brother's injustice. The situation was so painful that Mark oscillated between wanting nothing to do with the toxic money or his family, and the intense desire to right this wrong and get his money. This massive drain left Mark with zero attention, energy, and desire to earn his own income. After working through the many aspects of this story with Tapping, he adopted a calmer, balanced outlook. He let his attorney deal with the court case, removed himself from all emotionally charged battles and conversations with family, and quickly found a good job. He also found peace.

Recognizing any toxic money you depend on and taking steps to clear the connection to negative emotions will transform your life far beyond just your money situation. That said, this could be the most difficult kind of money dysfunction to change, if you think it's necessary to stay in your situation to survive. It's extremely difficult to step out of a codependent relationship or a battle over money and feel completely free to start creating more. In many cases, people believe as Mark did—that if their situation remains dire, there's more hope that they will be given their due.

Clearly understanding what emotions and beliefs each type of money triggers is critical to making changes in your financial picture. When you're aware of emotions you may have and recognize your specific blocks, you can begin to clear them with laser focus and achieve the best results. Clearing specific blocks around all five areas of money will not only completely shift what you create and attract in your financial picture but it will also begin a massive transformation in the power you feel over your life. Don't underestimate the level at which your life will change when you begin to clear your blocks. You may feel as though you're focusing specifically on money, but the overall impact will be much, much more significant in your life.

Create Your Personal Money Map: A quick exercise revealing how you are programmed in all five categories of money so you can laserfocus your progress www.TappingIntoWealth.com/Video3

4

HOW DO YOU *REALLY* FEEL ABOUT MONEY? (NOT ABUNDANCE—MONEY!)

Ow badly do you want more money? Enough to look inside yourself to find what's blocking the flow of money to you? Enough to face emotions that have been buried for many years? Enough to be honest with yourself about how you really feel about money, every time you deal with it? We're inundated with financial books, TV shows, and workshops; yet many people continue to wonder, "Why don't I have more money?" Even with all the available resources and tools that could change one's financial picture, a vast majority of people never implement what they learn because actions are driven by how they feel right now. How you want to feel in the future has no bearing.

Feelings power actions. They have precedence over logic, practicality, discipline, and great ideas. If you feel neutral about something, then logic, reason, and choice guide actions. But if you don't, your emotions commandeer what you do or don't do. Memories, beliefs, and programming about money create strong feelings that drive every action you take and motivate you to avoid taking actions that involve increasing your income and savings and lowering your debt. That's why many financial experts are fantastic money managers for their clients, but amass their own significant debt or live hand to mouth. Since they're neutral about their clients' money, they're logical—even brilliant. But it's the opposite with their own money.

It's incredibly important to make the effort to recognize your feelings about money in an honest way, since it's more comfortable to ignore them. Once you acknowledge your feelings, the power to earn more begins to shift to your control. First, you need to find any emotional pain you may have that's specific to money, and clear it. Unfortunately, most people don't want to look for this pain and wouldn't know what to do if they found it. But this critical first step is truly where the transformation in your money situation begins—and the key to increasing your wealth.

My first intention is to help you recognize your emotions related to money and how they're connected to—and creating—your financial picture. Your true feelings, which are often just below your consciousness, determine almost every aspect of how you make and handle money.

Testing Your Money Emotions

Answering the question "Why don't I have more money?" requires you to look below the surface of your conscious feelings, often way below, to discover your true emotions about it. The first exercise allows you to take proactive steps to recognize those that drive your financial picture. After all, you can't change what you're not aware of. Try this with a very open mind so you can begin to recognize the truth about why you don't have more money.

Exercise for Testing Money Emotions

Write your current income—the actual number you earn right now—in big letters on a blank paper. If you're trying to start or build a business or switch from a mediocre job to the job you'd love to have, write just the income you'd earn in your dream job—the one you want to expand the most, the career or work you want as your biggest source of income. Even if you work a part-time job to help pay bills, just include income sources you want to expand.

Focus on the number you wrote down and say out loud, "I'm earning (or will earn) ____ per week/month." Even at this point in the exercise, some people start feeling uncomfortable about that black-and-white number. Now look at it and say aloud, "It's not enough!" Take some deep breaths and allow yourself to feel what happens in your body when you say that.

Note how true this statement—"It's not enough"—feels to you. Does it create an intense feeling in your body? Write down those feelings and measure them on a scale of 1 to 10, with 1 being calm and 10 representing the most intense, uncomfortable emotion when you say, "It's not enough!"

I've done this exercise with many thousands of people from around the world, individually and in groups. The overwhelming feedback is that saying "It's not enough!" feels very true. Many explain they're trying to earn more or are frustrated that their income isn't enough to support them. Those who've tried to start a new business or have been running their own for several years feel particularly bad about their income and say: "I feel anxiety"; "I feel panic"; "I feel sadness"; "I feel shame"; "I feel anger." These negative emotions all contribute to the problem.

For example, Jean and Carol were friends who invested in their dream of owning a natural foods store. They were avid followers of the Law of Attraction, read positive thinking books, attended workshops, created vision boards showing their thriving business, and hung a sign with a million dollars as their goal. However, after working long hours for eleven years, business was flat. They barely earned enough to support their personal lives. When asked to share emotions that surfaced about their personal take-home income, Jean and Carol became resistant, especially about voicing "It's not enough." They explained that focusing on negatives went against their beliefs. They preferred to reset their million-dollar goal and try harder to believe it would come.

I gently explained the importance of finding and clearing negativity. Otherwise, being positive is an uphill battle. I assured them that this process would create the opposite of negatives—a much higher positive vibe. They tried being strong and positive for each other, but emotions poured out as Jean and Carol recognized how much sadness and disappointment was behind their cheerful façades. Their dream business triggered a constellation of painful negative feelings they fought daily: constant fear and anxiety about making ends meet, sadness about trips they couldn't afford to take, guilt about their families who supported them, disillusioned hopes and dreams, and frustration and hopelessness about improvement.

Jean and Carol trusted me enough to refocus on the take-home pay from their business. They were surprised by the intensity of their emotional pain caused by money and how hard they fought those feelings. They finally recognized why they never analyzed or discussed business revenue and income openly or spent time strategizing on business growth. Facing it was too emotionally charged. Acknowledging it was a relief.

EMOTIONAL FINANCES

Your income is the largest stream of money flowing into your life, so how you feel about it really matters. That's why facing the fact that you don't have enough to support you or your dreams is difficult. The reality is, whether you face the real emotional impact head on or ignore it, it remains present on some level, like a heavy burden you can't shake. Many people experience intense anxiety and racing thoughts about money during quiet moments, like bedtime. Any time money comes up in some way, the emotional impact is felt, even if you try to squelch or control it. Fear, anxiety, panic, sadness, anger, and frustration are triggered at some level in your body and nervous system.

When these emotions get strong, they activate the stress response, also called the fight-or-flight response, which attaches an additional heaping of pain. You may feel it right now and want to stop this exercise. The fight-or-flight response is an inborn, primitive reaction designed to do one thing—give you physiological readiness to fight for your life or run to safety. It's a powerful drive that intensifies and reinforces feelings that create a negative feedback loop. In modern life, we don't fight for survival physically, so the impact of this response only hampers us mentally. It's well documented in literature that when it's activated, thinking narrows, problem-solving ability decreases, creative thinking is obstructed, and thoughts race or become fuzzy. Energy floods your body, and muscle tense, as your mind goes into survival mode, scanning the horizon for danger. You can't access all your brilliance when this is happening.

Every time you get paid, or look at your checkbook, or pay bills, or thoughts related to finances cross your mind, negative emotions about money can trigger your entire nervous system into the fight-or-flight response. Since this is painful, it elicits two reactions. First, you avoid dealing with and thinking about money as much as possible and put almost no energy, time, and focus into your money situation. Second, when you must deal with money, you'll have a survival mind-set. The negative emotions leave you less able to think, plan, and act creatively, brilliantly, or efficiently. Your inborn survival response convinces your brain:

> *I don't need amazing creative ideas and certainly don't need math right now. I need all my energy, my fighting and running muscles ready, and my mind to look at one field of view, racing and ready, looking for more danger on the horizon, ready to go, go, go.*

If you don't have the level of money you say you want, the truth is that emotions related to money are interfering with your ability to earn a lot more and handle what you have in ways that grow your assets. Studies report that even thinking one negative thought can trigger your body to release cortisol, a hormone known as a marker for stress levels. Stress keeps you off the track you say you want to be on. Then again, your physiology responds to feeling happy, enthusiastic, and positive with feel-good chemicals that put your mind in the right place for getting what you want, inspiring actions that create more money.

Even if you have a good income, old issues can trigger severe negative emotions that keep you from enjoying what you have and hurt your well-being. For example, when I met Kathryn, she earned a good living as a consultant in the biotech industry and had a great retirement plan. But she admitted to having constant anxiety about money. When I asked her to write down her income, she immediately felt fear and anxiety. A familiar phrase repeated in her head: "Right around the corner, the other shoe is going to drop." As she said it, her eyes welled with tears and her voice began to shake as old memories surfaced.

She explained, "This is just how it is, and has been this way since childhood." Kathryn believed that no matter how much you make, there will always be something that falls out of the sky to take your money—a bill, car repair, injury, taxes, etc. And she believed it would take every last cent she had. To her, no matter how much you make, you can never rest, relax, or stop worrying because there will never be enough. As she shared this, Kathryn was resigned to this being her inescapable fate. Her emotions escalated as she recalled childhood memories of watching her mother live with a black cloud of worry and fear from the same living-hand-to-mouth mentality, and viewing her life through the lens of just getting by.

Regardless of how much Kathryn's income and her level of financial security with her husband increased over the years, she experienced constant anxiety and insomnia from worrying about when the other shoe would drop and eat up all her income and maybe even her savings. The effect on her health was profound. Worrying about money was the primary reason she was on medication for anxiety and insomnia. After addressing this with Tapping, Kathryn reported sleeping for twelve straight hours that night. She laughed about how her husband eventually woke her to make sure she was okay. As her stress and obsessive worry faded away, she was able to fall asleep easily and finally enjoy the financial security she worked hard to create.

Being in the fight-or-flight state leaves you less resourceful in taking action. You might pray or work harder or try to use the Law of Attraction to manifest more money, but what has the biggest impact on your ability to change your financial circumstances is how you really feel when thinking about your income. This is because your feelings drive your thinking and actions. Ignoring negative emotions won't make them go away. This is where Tapping makes a powerful difference, since it literally turns off the fight-or-flight response. All those negative emotions work against your quest to increase your bottom line. Tapping is an effective antidote.

TURNING OFF THE FIGHT-OR-FLIGHT RESPONSE

You can talk about abundance, prosperity, infinite possibility, and miracles in an attempt to override your true feelings about money, but you might as well be reading a grocery list for all the good it will do. Even if you seek help from energetic healers or study spiritual teachings or explore self-development books and classes, you won't be open to the infinite possibility that exists in every moment or great ideas sparked from within you if you're in survival mode.

You have a storehouse of genius that could rise up and help you to think of many ways to double, quadruple, or at least slightly increase your income. It doesn't matter where you start. What's important is to let the ideas and brilliance in you surface. Unfortunately, it can't happen if your mentality is, "I just want to survive." Often people tell me, "I *just* need enough to get by," "I *just* want to pay my bills," "I *just* want to be able to take my kids on one vacation." I just, I just, I just! Do you recognize the survival mode in that? It blocks access to bigger thinking and your ability to use tools like the Law of Attraction.

It's important to note that "just surviving" means different things to different people, depending on their experiences. If you were raised in a lower to even upper middle-class family, and experienced some scarcity in childhood, or there was barely enough to get by and not much for extras, it's more probable that you'll have the "it's not enough" fear or anxiety reaction about your income, since it brings up those memories. If you lived in survival mode growing up, you're even more likely to be in it now. Living from paycheck to paycheck is survival mode. Struggling to keep up your mortgage payments is survival mode.

There are unlimited opportunities to use your energy to attract money or manifest unexpected miracles. But you can't take advantage of them if you're "just" trying to get through each day, "just" managing to pay bills, or "just" keeping yourself going. No matter how much you want to use tools you see working for others, they won't work while you're struggling to just survive. If you want more money, it's critical to recognize survival mode in yourself and measure it by paying close attention to its intensity. Then do Tapping exercises to clear what keeps you stuck.

When you use Tapping to turn off fear, anxiety, anger, and sadness, the intensity lowers in minutes. The number that represents the income you wrote on the page earlier stays the same; yet the emotional response to the number drastically changes for the better. Diffusing negative emotions with Tapping allows you to look at your income number, even if it's still not enough, and at least feel neutral instead of negative. Or you might think, "That's where I am now but I'm excited and determined to make life better." After doing some Tapping, thoughts of money will stop immobilizing you.

As Tapping turns off the fight-or-flight response and neutralizes negative emotions, hope, excitement, and curiosity reappear with stronger intensity. When there's possibility, energy rises through your system and you're willing to use it to focus your brilliant creative mind on a whole new wealth reality. This vibe makes it easy and fun to take real action! When your positive emotions match your intentions, you're truly in a position to increase wealth and achieve big goals.

That's exactly what happened with Jean and Carol after they Tapped to neutralize the fear, anxiety, and sadness they felt about their income. They said, almost in unison, "This is just where we are right now. We can change this, right?" They both felt ideas brewing, and excitement filled the room. First, they wrote a new income goal that was a healthy step up from where they'd been stuck for years, but not one million. This goal excited and challenged them. They brainstormed on ideas for building their business and committed to make changes and measure the impact of those changes on their bottom line, which they'd never done.

Several months after they tried and tested many ideas, several new opportunities appeared. As they shared their growth vision with colleagues and vendors, people lined up to support them. By collaborating, they created successful open house events that brought people to their store and created excitement. Their income rose for the first time as they planned more changes.

The simple exercise of writing down your income and saying "It's not enough," illustrates the big conflict between money goals and what really happens when you think about your financial picture. The fight-or-flight response greatly hinders everything you should consider doing to increase your income. Even if you're not feeling desperate about money, thoughts about it subconsciously trigger old survival programming that still runs in your thoughts, over and over, unless you consciously change it.

Now it's time for you to see how Tapping works. I'll lead you in your first round to reduce anxiety and any fight-or-flight response to your income. As you tap on the points, loudly voice as honestly as possible all your feelings about it. Emotions may feel stronger in the beginning when you're new to it. As you Tap on feelings, you'll start to shift into a true openness that inspires great ideas, excitement, and enthusiasm about what's possible. Being able to recognize and shift how you really feel about money is a powerful first step to changing your money situation.

Now let's try some Tapping to clear negative emotions. Take a minute to restate out loud, "It's not enough." Use the script but feel free to replace the words with your own feelings and memories when possible. The script is a guide. You can use it as a reference to write your own. It may take several rounds or more before the emotions have no impact on you. Tap on your list of feelings and thoughts triggered by saying, "My income is not enough."

TAPPING SCRIPT FOR EMOTIONS
ABOUT INCOME

Say the following phrases aloud while tapping on the karate chop point on the pinkie side of your hand:

Even though the truth is I try to be positive, this number is just not enough. And I really feel that right in my stomach; it is depressing. It is scary. It is hopeless and I am really disappointed. I totally honor all of these real feelings and I am so open to healing them because this is a conflict.

Even though this money just isn't enough, I am going to accept all my awful feelings about that—this hopeless feeling, this deep shame. Shouldn't I be ashamed? All my disappointment and all my fears. Oh my God! What if it never changes? I am really feeling the pain of money.

Even though my money just isn't enough—I am just not earning enough and that is the truth—I honor who I am anyway and all this heavy emotion about money. It feels so disappointing, depressing, it is a battle.

Continue Tapping through all the points, using the following phrases (refer to the diagram in chapter 2 if you need to review where the Tapping points are):

This feeling in my stomach *** Oh! I don't want to look at this *** My income just isn't enough *** I try to be positive *** I have been being positive for years *** And it is still not enough *** It hasn't ever been enough *** It is really scary *** It feels hopeless *** Disappoint-

(continued)

ing *** And shameful *** It is *just* not enough *** Panic *** Fear ***
Depression *** Anger *** Every time I think about money *** Every
time I see my income *** It is really hard to be grateful *** When I
feel so bad *** It is just not enough.

Take a nice deep breath. Now look at your income number again
and voice aloud, "It's not enough." The statement may still be very true,
but measure again how intense your feelings and reactions are now on
the scale of 1 to 10. This is a great way to see how far you've shifted or
if you need to Tap through the round again. When the emotional intensity comes down on the scale to a 1, you can get to the other side
and go from fear, sadness, and disappointment to empowerment and a
whole new vibe about your income. So get positive! When you disconnect your programmed response, you can instill a new one. You have
the space and ability to choose a new way to feel great, excited, interested, and enthusiastic about money.

Let's Tap again, but this time instilling a powerful positive affirmation to shift and reframe how you feel about money.

SAY THE FOLLOWING PHRASES ALOUD WHILE TAPPING ON THE KARATE CHOP POINT:

Even though my income still isn't enough, I am totally open to the
millions of ways that money can show up for me.

Even though this isn't what I wanted it to be, I recognize in the
present moment that I am just looking at a result on paper, from my
past. But in this present moment, I am a powerful manifestor. So I
am changing my vibration about money. I am totally open to all the
ways money can start showing up for me. And everything I need, I

am now attracting to me. To allow more money into my life, I am now attracting ideas, inspirations, actions, people, circumstances—anything I need to allow money to show up for me. I am opening up my vibration about money by saying one simple word—Yes! I am now saying *yes* to money!

Now Tap through the points, using the following phrases or your own:

Looking at money used to make me angry *** Or fearful and depressed *** Now when I look at money, I just say *yes* *** I actually love receiving money *** It is really fun to get money *** I actually am grateful for the money I have right now *** I am now open *** To receiving any kind of (*legal*) money *** I am saying *yes* to all sorts and forms of money *** Cash, check, or charge *** I am saying *yes* to money *** A whole new vibration about money.

I am letting go of fear and depression *** I am letting go of shame and anger *** And I am now allowing *** The *real* me *** To resonate with money *** I really love money *** It is fun because I am good at what I do *** I really love earning money *** I love what I do *** I *am really* good at it *** And now I am open to receiving *** With one simple word *** Yes to money *** I am saying *yes* to money.

I am going to say *yes* to money *** All day long *** When I wake up in the morning *** When I go to sleep *** *Yes* to money *** Even when I dream, I am saying *yes* to money.

I love this vibration *** I love this vibration of receiving *** I am now receiving and welcoming *** More money *** Into my home *** Into my business *** Right into my hands *** I am so curious *** As to how it will show up.

And I am already feeling *** Excited *** And grateful *** For more money showing up.

Yes to money *** Thank you for money *** Open to receiving money *** All the way through me *** Mind, body, and soul.

PERSONALIZING A LACK OF MONEY

Here's another exercise to find more clues about how you really feel about money. As bad as the fight-or-flight response triggered by your income can feel, what results from this exercise can bring up much darker stuff. This is the ruthless, negative self-talk we continually bombard ourselves with, leading to blame, judgment, recrimination, and punishment. It's a secondary effect of how you really feel about money, but its impact can be even more powerfully damaging. This next exercise will help raise your consciousness about your inner self-talk so you can really start moving forward.

Exercise for Personalizing a Lack of Money

Look at the income number you wrote down and say, "It's not enough." Then fill in the blank in this sentence: "This means I'm _____." It can be hard. I'd venture to guess you're beating yourself up on your own anyway. List as many answers as you can think of. Keep it on your mind as you go through your day and add to your list.

There's judgment and a process that occurs in your head whenever you consider income that isn't quite enough to support you in the way you want, often accompanied by an inner dialogue on what your income means about you personally. Your inner critic, or self-hater, can fill in the blank with some of the most painful self-recriminations I've heard. For example:

- "This means I'm a loser."
- "This means I'm a failure."

- "This means I'm letting people down, disappointing them, disappointing myself, because I don't have what it takes."
- "This means I can never get ahead because the world is stacked against me."

As you think about your income during this exercise, let what pops into your mind immediately come out. Be honest. Tune in to the intensity of your response, the words and emotions. Often people quickly recognize how powerfully negative this is. You can see it right there on the page! Once again, this exercise illustrates a conflict. Every time you think about your income, it triggers a cascade of not only fight-or-flight emotions, but also some pretty dark self-talk that sabotages positive progress.

For example, Bob was a single dad with two kids. His divorce left him broke because he willingly took on all the joint debt from his marriage. It left him feeling so low and disempowered that he splurged on a top-of-the-line snowmobile. He came to one of my workshops to learn why he couldn't set big income goals, and how to change it. But as we did goal-setting exercises, he kept getting stuck and actually started to feel physically ill. I asked him what came up. Each time Bob tried to consider the possibility of earning more money, his inner voice said loud and clear, "You don't deserve it, you loser!"

He choked up and explained, "The reality is, I've totally mismanaged my money. I've acted like an idiot, let myself get taken advantage of, and put myself in debt." I asked, "What does that mean about you? What is your judgment about someone like that?" He answered simply. "I'm a loser and deserve to be embarrassed and humiliated right now. I'm a bad father because I can't afford a nice place for my children to live in." Everyone in the room felt Bob's pain. It was clear that any time he thought about his money situation—past, present, or future—he replayed *exactly* what it meant about him: Loser. Humiliation. Bad father.

Negative self-talk sabotages even the best intentions for actions you can take to make more money. Imagine a seven-year-old boy playing baseball. It's his turn to hit, but as he walks to the plate, a very harsh coach stands over him, screaming the kinds of critical things you wrote down about how money makes you feel about yourself. Picture this scenario and think about how that child feels after hearing it:

- Will he continue to be excited and enthusiastic about playing baseball after negatives are hurled at him?
- Can he perform well with his coach screaming at him that way?

You are that child when it comes to your self-talk about your income. Negative self-talk reinforces a strong connection between money and the way you see yourself in relationship to it. Unless you do something to clear your self-criticism, thinking about money can bring up all the horrible, shameful, awful, failing feelings. It doesn't have to be that way! It's more pleasant and productive to free your mind so that you can generate ideas and enthusiastically anticipate doubling or quadrupling your wealth and take action to make it happen. But how can that happen with so much negativity tied to money and negative emotions blocking it? The fight-or-flight emotions and the cascade of painful negative self-talk reflect what most people do:

- Totally avoid dealing with their money
- Never set goals around their income
- Never spend the time and energy to have a full handle on their finances
- Never try to get a full handle on their business income

I've lost count of how many self-employed people and small-business owners tell me, "I don't know how much I actually earn from my business." Examining the root of money blocks is too painful to face. It can seem easier to just live day to day, trying to just pay bills, praying no one gets sick, wishing for a miracle that creates a college fund for your kids, and hoping that if you ignore your finances, it will be okay. But it doesn't work that way. Until you clear your money blocks, nothing changes. As uncomfortable or painful as it may be, it's imperative to identify and relive old experiences by feeling the emotions they trigger in order to get to the other side of them.

When you Tap and voice negative self-talk, you don't reinforce it as some may think. Instead, Tapping completely changes the dynamics of those feelings! The big emotional charge from negative self-talk will dissipate and the words will no longer feel true. As shocking as it may seem to initially voice negative words directed at yourself, the shift in feelings, thinking, and perspective is truly magnificent—an unbelievably powerful upside to facing it. This release is a loving gift from a few minutes of Tapping, one that will transform your feelings about money and your willingness to spend the time, energy, and attention on everything you can do to expand your income. That's how you get more money!

When Bob voiced his painful inner dialogue about what money meant about him, most of the packed room acknowledged, "Me too!" That gave him the courage to Tap. We Tapped loudly, voicing all the negative self-talk as if it were the irrefutable truth, since that's how we say it to ourselves. A weight lifted from the room. I asked Bob to restate his painful sentence out loud. It sounded monotone, like reciting a recipe, followed by, "That's not true! I made mistakes but I am smart and a *really* good father." His face changed and his voice had strong resolve and determination. Bob couldn't wait to tear into his goal work and was a total inspiration for the other attendees. Several months later, Bob sold his snowmobile, consolidated his debt, moved into a great apartment, and was interviewing for a better job that would allow more time with his kids.

Now do Tapping for your negative self-talk. Look at your list from the exercise above, "This means I'm_____," and note the intensity of emotions as you say that, and how true it feels on a scale of 1 to 10, with 1 being not true at all and 10 being 100 percent true. Use words you relate to.

TAPPING SCRIPT FOR NEGATIVE SELF-TALK

Say the following phrases aloud while tapping on the karate chop point:

Even though my income isn't enough, I totally blame myself. I am a loser. That's what my income means. I should have been able to fix this. I should be doing better. Clearly I haven't done enough and I am going to love and accept myself as totally unacceptable.

Even though my income is just not enough and I know what that means, it is all on me. I should have done it better. I should be doing it right. I am totally missing something. I am failing. I honor who I am anyway.

Even though this income right here on my paper means only one thing—I am screwing up. I am failing. This number defines me. I accept who I am anyway, even though I really don't because I should have done it better.

Now Tap through the points, using the following phrases or your own:

All this heavy self-judgment *** I should have done it better *** I keep screwing up *** I must be missing something *** Oh my God! I've got to figure this out *** This number means *** I am losing ***

I am failing *** I am not doing it right *** It is so heavy *** I feel all the guilt *** So stupid *** It is so embarrassing *** If people knew what I earned *** I would be humiliated *** It is all me *** It has got to be *** I am doing it wrong *** And every time I think that thought *** I tell the universe *** I don't deserve *** And it feels so heavy *** That I get stuck *** And my view of abundance *** And possibility ** * Shrinks down small.

Should have done it better *** All my fault *** I am failing *** Every time I think those thoughts *** I contract *** I get stuck *** I push myself lower *** I push my deserving lower *** All these self-judgmental thoughts *** I am open to seeing them for what they are *** Thoughts running in my head *** Habitual thoughts running in my head *** I am just going to be open to the idea *** That I have always done my best *** And I actually deserve right now *** That would feel really different.

Take a nice deep breath and say, "That means I'm_____." Notice how much less intense and true it feels. Take a second to measure again how true it feels now and compare it to the number you felt before Tapping. If your "it feels true" number is still above a 2, repeat the rounds of Tapping with words that resonate with your feelings until it feels like they don't fit you anymore.

After your negative self-talk dissipates, get positive! Choose self-talk that supports you and your goals for being a better money manager. Now let's do some positive Tapping!

POSITIVE TAPPING FOR
SELF-TALKS ABOUT INCOME

Say the following phrases aloud while Tapping on the karate chop point:

Even though my income still looks really bad on paper, the truth is, I am not a loser. I have made some mistakes, maybe I have played small, but I have what it takes to make a change.

Even though this current income does not reflect my value, that does not define me! I will not be defined. I have more potential in me than I have seen yet. Instead, I honor my brilliance and I am open to more of that, more of my own brilliance.

Now Tap through the points as you say each of these phrases, or your own:

Looking at my income was making me think *** *Loser* *** Boy, is *that helpful!* *** *Not!* *** I do have a challenge here *** And I am going to rise to the challenge *** That is what a winner does *** I am not even sure how yet *** But I am setting my sights higher *** I can do this! *** The truth is I am pretty smart *** I am grateful for my brains! *** I can learn anything *** And I have accomplished a lot of things in my life *** Some of them were really hard, but I did it *** I am grateful for my persistence.

I've done some things that were scary *** But I pushed through and found the courage *** I am grateful for my courage *** I have made lots of mistakes *** And each one has made me smarter *** Each one has taught me lessons *** Each one has made me savvy *** I am grateful for my mistakes! *** All this supports me in this new vision *** My income is just *where* I am right now *** Not *who* I am! *** As I remember I am the hero of my story *** I am the hero of *my life*.

   I get to move forward growing my income *** With confidence, with courage, with clarity *** I totally honor who I am right now! *** And who I am becoming *** I honor my income and the challenge it gives me *** A challenge—I *accept*! *** With honor, with brilliance, with all of me! *** I am so-o-o-o going for it!

Take a deep breath. Can you feel that you've shifted from the extreme of negative self-talk (and the child with a ruthless coach) to neutral? Can you remember your truth? Recall your strengths, gifts, courage, and desire to achieve. Does it sound like a self-pep-talk? That's exactly what it is and infinitely more powerful after dissipating negative self-talk. If you still have negative feelings, do the rounds again until you feel calmer. Notice how much more energy, enthusiasm, and willingness you have to grow your income by remembering that you're the hero in your story—much better than feeling like a loser! Energy, enthusiasm, and willingness become inspired and determined actions. And actions get results!

Your Daily Shift to Creating and Attracting More Income: A quick Tapping routine to use daily, focused on the shift to earning and receiving more! www.TappingIntoWealth.com/Video4

5

YOUR EARLIEST VIEW OF MONEY PARADIGM

D o you think your feelings about money stem from your current financial situation? Wrong! You might assume that your
negative emotions are a natural reaction to the frustration of
not having as much money as you'd like. But in reality, your current
feelings reflect how you were programmed to feel about money, usually
in childhood. Often, this determines your financial state more than
any other factor.

This concept is a total reversal of the cause and effect that appears
to be your reality. You may think that a million external factors created
all aspects of your money situation. Many seem to land on you as random problems, mix-ups, expenses, and events beyond your control. But
what if they aren't random? What if you somehow created every part
of your money picture—even seemingly external factors—to re-create
conditions that match how you're programmed to feel about money?

I believe you create external factors that impact your money picture
according to a master money plan of sorts, which is unconsciously set
by your early experiences. Your emotions about money came first, pro-

grammed from your earliest associations with it. Everything related to your current financial picture came from those emotions. It may seem ridiculous to believe that your view of money began long ago. After all, if you're not happy with your finances now, logic says the current unhappiness creates your negative emotions. But logic aside, to increase wealth, you must find the true origin of those emotions so you can clear them.

Underlying emotions from the past create a sort of template for your dissatisfaction today. In chapter 4, you did exercises to determine how you really feel about money and identified any anxiety, fear, panic, sadness, anger, or frustration connected to your income. In this chapter, I'll help you begin to trace the roots of some of those feelings so you can recognize and release your blocks to increased wealth.

Picturing Childhood Memories

The biggest source of programmed feelings about money is what I call your "earliest money paradigm"—the ingrained patterns and experiences from long ago that created a model for what money means to you today. This paradigm creates a template that you will re-create unless you clear it. My goal is to guide you to amazing "aha" moments by doing exercises to reveal this paradigm and show how it continues to trigger negative emotions that feed an inability to brighten your financial picture. You need to not only see and feel old experiences around money but also face the intensity and power it has over you now.

Many self-help educators emphasize the importance of recognizing your limiting beliefs, fears, and paradigms around money. Yet knowing you have blocks can leave you more frustrated if you also know your programming is unconscious. It creates questions and concerns that don't have obvious answers:

- How can I clear blocks I'm not conscious of?
- How can I identify limiting beliefs or programming if I don't know what they are?

I want to help you identify yours so you can clear what hinders your pursuit of more money! My process makes the unconscious very conscious. Once you see your earliest paradigm with clarity, it's harder to delude yourself about why you don't have more money and you'll feel more empowered to improve your financial situation for good. Reaching the "aha" moments that make this happen requires recognizing and acknowledging negative childhood memories that can be painful at first but lead to long-term financial rewards.

Tapping clears a lot of the programming that created your paradigm around money and adds a strong component to the work you do to increase wealth. Your biggest "aha" moment will be the first time you recognize the origin and reason for the entire pattern from which you operate regarding your money. That opens the door to the most significant aspect of the transformation you can achieve. Start by doing this exercise:

Exercise for Earliest View of Money Paradigm

Sit with your eyes closed and picture yourself around age six or seven. Take a nice deep breath and let your mind fill in details of that picture. Get to the point where you can see what you're wearing. Some people worry they're making up a picture or remembering a photograph. It's okay. The important thing is to let your mind paint a detailed picture in whatever way it can of you as a child.

Next paint your parents into the image. Picture them talking about and dealing with money or bills. See that whole picture.

- *What's going on in it?*
- *How do your parents seem to feel about money?*
- *What are they doing?*
- *What are they saying?*

Now look at you in the picture. You're just a child, but are down-loading all that data about money, working hard, scarcity, disempowerment, and fear. What are you feeling in the picture? Note how well the feelings and challenges your parents have about money match how you currently operate around it in your life. Usually it's shockingly similar.

As you picture your parents, observe your personal history with money. What did you see or hear as a child? The feelings around money that you observed back then created your current money picture. Note very specifically:

- Was there worry, anxiety, or any traumas in relation to money?
- Did a parent lose a job, or did you have a comfortable lifestyle until something painful happened to change it?
- Was there a big betrayal centered on money?
- Was one parent excessive with money in any way: spending, saving, or refusing to earn it?
- Was there never enough?
- Was there plenty of money in your childhood but also tremendous family pressure and control regarding who you had to be to get it?
- Did your parents never talk about money so you learned nothing about managing it, but only thought of it as a taboo subject?
- Did you hear things like, "You'll be who we say you will be," or "You don't need to go to college. Just marry well"?

- Do you remember witnessing arguments or anger related to money?

Write: *Get all the details down on paper that you remember about this money picture and the feelings money created when you were young. Think about this over the next few days and if something else comes up, write it down too. These details will help you find and clear blocks. Don't limit observations to what you think is important. Note everything!*

If your parents were often angry about or fighting over money issues, or feeling disempowered about finances, you may associate money with anger or conflict, which can make you subconsciously not want too much and sabotage your goals of having it. This is particularly true if you felt like you were in the middle of arguments or caused your parents' money problems. Hundreds of people have shared that as children they felt responsibility, and in some cases were told, "You caused our financial burden." A hot-button issue for some occurred when a divorce or separation in childhood caused fighting over who would pay for what. If providing child support for you triggered heated money arguments, then at some level, you'll always associate money with anger, fighting, and guilt, and get rid of yours fast, regardless of how much you earn.

Often the paradigm that contributes to your situation today isn't obvious. For example, Mary saw her childhood as good and stable. As an adult, she earned a great living but never saved one cent. Money came in and right back out with not a penny to spare. Despite her great income, she was always anxious about money, as if she was one paycheck away from ruin. Mary had no cushion if she lost her job, or freedom to do much more than make ends meet. She worried about it a lot.

We looked at her earliest money paradigm. Her father earned a great salary but had nine kids, and her parents lived paycheck to paycheck. There was just enough and they were happy and grateful for that. But they worried constantly and stretched every dollar to make ends meet. Mary's parents often stated that they were proud and willing to sacrifice so their kids could have more. She quickly recognized she was reliving this paradigm and was surprised to feel shame about wanting more than her proud and sacrificing parents had.

Shouldn't she be happy with what she had? They had no extra money but were good, happy people. Mary also realized she'd never considered the possibility of creating savings, security, and wealth. Her reality was that money would always be hand to mouth. Since she believed it was impossible to save, she never tried. With that major limiting belief uncovered, Mary was free to create the security she desired. She bought a book on personal finance and executed a plan. Within a year, she has $10,000 in her savings account.

If your money history has any negative beliefs, it creates an unbelievable amount of chaos and complication in how you deal with finances. You'll associate money with anger, betrayal, abandonment, fear, and survival. So note everything in your picture, everything you visualize happening. Get all these details on paper and don't question it. Just write it down for now.

My Parents/My Money Model

If you objectively compare how your parents felt about and dealt with money to your current patterns, it can be a pretty eerie match if you pay close attention. Even if you vowed to *never* be anything like your parents, you are still shaped by them. Your beliefs about who you are, your value, your view of the nature of money, and how hard you have to work for it come from your earliest money paradigm that's picked up from your family—your tribe of origin, as we say. You may have heard positive or negative attitudes about people with more money than they had. Was it okay to have more, or did your parents consider those with much bigger incomes evil or corrupt? That can subconsciously set limitations on how much you feel you should earn.

Children also pick up different kinds of pride around money from parents: pride in not having much and still having a happy life, or pride in having more than others. Parents instill in us beliefs about the world and how it operates for people in the financial circumstances you were in. You might remember hearing:

- "People in our family never get ahead."
- "We may not have much, but we have what matters."
- "We may never be rich, but at least we're good people."
- "We make good employees, but can't run a business."

Look at those beliefs and your own. As a child, you had no choice but to absorb all the family's "truths" about the nature of money, wealth, opportunity, and hard work. You couldn't raise your hand and say, "Hey, Mom and Dad, stop! It doesn't have to be this way. You can create your own abundance reality." If you tried, it would have challenged your parents' view of the world. That would have likely triggered some kind of repercussion—an argument, criticism, or review of all the "evidence" until you acquiesced to you parents' way of seeing things. To challenge the paradigm is to challenge your parents; that makes life uncomfortable and leads us to the most important piece of understanding your family's money paradigm.

CHILDHOOD VOWS

As eye-opening as it can be to see their family's money paradigm, people often think that it does not have much impact or control over their current adult life. "How could it? Why would it?" they ask. The implications go far beyond just absorbing views of money and wealth. We actually make unconscious vows about these views that have the power to limit and impoverish ourselves for a lifetime.

As children, we have a built-in, reptilian brain, survival instincts that focus on being accepted and safe inside our families. If someone were alone in the wilderness because his tribe had kicked him out, he wouldn't survive long. In modern times, this powerful instinct to survive physically applies more to emotional survival, which drives us to figure out how to get the most safety, love, nurturing, and positive attention, and how best to avoid criticism, danger, physical pain, and rejection.

This instinct to survive and thrive in your tribe is so hardwired and strong that children take a vow to ensure the highest possibility of success—to be loyal to their family's paradigm. This encompasses all aspects of the "who you are" and "how you feel about things" dynamics learned from your family, including how empowered or disempowered you feel about money. It also applies to what kind of person you are in relation to your level of success, income, education, wealth, and what's possible for "people like me." Typically, you're not aware of this vow.

Interestingly, there are other, opposing vows from childhood—to never be anything like your family and to rebel against their beliefs— that are often made deliberately. The primitive survival instinct has another aspect beyond personal responses—survival and evolution of the species. That instinct hardwires you to want to grow, differentiate yourself from the tribe, think differently, and rebel. So you end up with two opposing vows regarding your family's paradigm. First, you vow to be loyal to it in order to fit in, never surpass your tribe or parents, and be good according to family standards. At the same time, you vow to rebel against that paradigm, reject its limitations, and never be like your family. These opposing vows operate within us simultaneously and drive our unconscious behavior in many areas of life in competing directions.

For example, you may specifically remember that you vowed to never be poor like your parents. That might have driven you to far exceed their income and success. But eventually, the vow to never surpass your tribe can create actions and behavior that sabotage your efforts, landing you back in the exact paradigm you vowed never to be in. This process leaves thousands of entrepreneurs and the many people who are self-employed stunned, devastated, and disillusioned, wondering how everything went so wrong.

In short, the vow of loyalty to your family's money paradigm causes you to limit money and success to stay in line with it. You restrict how you earn, manage, and save money, no matter how brilliant, talented, or educated you are. This vow makes you play small, not ask for much, and doubt your value. The vow of rebellion against that paradigm pushes you to consciously strive to surpass and break free of it while you unconsciously sabotage your success. You deliberately hinder how you earn, manage, and save money. The conflict between your instinct and the vow causes cycles of ups and downs: growth and momentum that suddenly turn to loss, betrayal, failure, and disappointment.

To see the vow of loyalty, pay attention to your feelings as you look at your parents in your picture. Even if you don't like what you see or disagree with how your parents did things, you might still feel sympathy or compassion for their struggle, particularly for the main breadwinner—for example: "My father worked so hard but never got a break," or "Mom sacrificed so much to give us what we needed and had little for herself." You might even feel it's unfair that they never felt empowered or lived their dreams. These feelings come from the loyalty vow. Even if you're angry looking back, there's often residual sadness if your parent was a good person and had to work hard for just enough money to survive.

The innate drive to be loyal to family means you'll re-create the same limitations, striving, working, and sacrificing with very little reward, and honor your parents with thoughts like, "They sacrificed so much for their children, but never enjoyed security and money. It would be wrong, disloyal, and selfish for me to have what they missed out on!" Their set point for earning, security, hard work, achievement, and disappointment becomes yours. You may consciously wish for more, as they did. But if you start moving beyond the set point of the paradigm, or even plan to, two powerful emotions will likely stop you—guilt and fear. Guilt comes from asking to enjoy everything your parents never got and wanting less struggle. If you achieve that, you show your parents it can be done and they did it wrong. You may fear surpassing your family since it could make you an outsider, different, and subject to potentially harsh judgment, mistrust, and rejection. You'll barely be conscious of these feelings, but they're powerful emotional drivers.

How does this happen? You limit yourself and the amount of money you work for in a million unconscious ways. Or, you expand how hard you must work for it to match your earliest family paradigm as an unconscious show of loyalty to your family. You may have an unconscious vow to never surpass them—to never outdo, try to stand out, be better than, or outshine your tribe. That's also true if you say, "If I made a million dollars, my parents would be proud of me." It doesn't matter what you feel consciously today. Early family memories drive your current financial picture.

Doug is a good example of this. We explored his money issues and how his father worked himself ragged to feed his family, care for his dying wife, and weather two business betrayals. His father never enjoyed a reward. This good and loving man died soon after he retired with a hard-earned nest egg. Doug sobbed for the unfairness of his father's life. In that moment, guilt from the loyalty vow emerged: "Who am I to get rewards when he didn't? I should be ashamed to want that." I asked what he could do to deserve rewards. He answered, "I'd have to work as hard as my father with as much adversity, challenge, and pain. Then maybe I'd earn the right to live his dream."

Doug's loyalty to his father kept his income low. On the other hand, many people make a vow of rebellion, with thoughts like, "Even as a child I consciously said, 'I'll never be like my parents. I'll do it differently.'" They charge forward, creating and manifesting money and success while being positive and believing it's possible to overcome the family paradigm. Yet, while they get lots of money and possessions, they self-sabotage with bad investments, overspending, and other actions that make them lose money, and cycle back to the same feelings their parents experienced. It's as though they push way up a mountain and create unbelievable things, but when money starts rolling in, they find themselves inexplicably reliving their parents' life. In this scenario, the vows of loyalty and rebellion operate simultaneously.

A vow of rebellion, to be nothing like your family—your tribe of origin—is also a vow to battle. You re-create your parents' reality and then battle against it, try to show you're better, prove you can outrun it and push past it. You believe you can do better. Then you sabotage yourself and the cycle begins again. I admit this isn't logical; yet people unconsciously exhibit this pattern over and over in their business. Take the case of Victor, who was 100 percent clear that he'd never be like his father and never be poor.

Victor discussed his father with disdain. "He was a good-for-nothing, abusive drunk, who never supported his family. I hated him and still do!" Throughout his life, he drove himself to create a multimillion-dollar business while being a loving husband and great father to his three children. However, when business took a sudden downturn, he became paralyzed with fear that he might lose it all. He became distant from his wife and kids, and seemed to freeze, watching as everything he built tumbled to the ground. Within months, he re-created the conditions of his childhood, with himself cast in the role of his father. His internal pain, self-loathing, and disappointment were overwhelming because as he said, "I vowed never to be like him, and now I am him. I can't support my family."

Look at this type of pattern in your own life and take full responsibility for it right now, since until this moment you had no idea it was running you. Now you know. Your family paradigm has more powerful control over your entire money picture than anything else in your life. Recognizing it begins to give that power back to you. I want you to have an "aha" moment about how you do this in your own life. When you clear the old paradigm, you get to control your financial steering wheel!

WEALTH SET POINTS

Your savings account is governed by the wealth set point you inherited from your family. It's an unwritten, unconscious number that's programmed into you without your knowing it, floating around in your unconscious mind, and flowing through all your actions. What is your set point? Well, you're already at it—the amount currently in your savings account. You've got the amount of wealth, security, safety, and everything involved in savings that you were programmed for. This set point is a number that makes you feel safe according to the loyalty vow to your family, even it if makes you feel very unsafe on the surface. That may sound really strange, since people usually feel more safe and secure when they have more savings and more scared and anxious when they don't. But this wealth set point connects to safety as it relates to your loyalty to your parents and family.

Your set point acts unconsciously like a kind of thermostat for your savings account. If you go beyond this number, you'll be considered outside the tribe and will make adjustments to bring the number back down. People who accumulate a lot more money than their programmed set point somehow manage to get rid of it. If they win a lottery, they may spend or lose it all. If your programming has negative associations about being rich and you suddenly have very substantial savings, your subconscious will guide you to all sorts of poor money management decisions to get rid of the extra money and come right back to your wealth set point.

Many people look at their savings account and think, "Well, this is just how it is. This is what I can afford." But none of that is true. Those beliefs were programmed into you, and the amount of your savings is the product of your wealth set point. When you raise it, your savings account will absolutely change. We'll work on this throughout the book.

CLEARING OLD PARADIGMS

Tapping to clear the emotion and energy around this early money paradigm is one of the most incredible gifts you can give yourself! It allows you to break patterns of limitation that come from a subconscious loyalty and to stop sabotaging what you manifest by rebelling against this family paradigm. When you clear the old money paradigm, you're free to choose your own satisfying one, without having to battle the old one, or prove you can be different from your parents, or stay in the old paradigm out of misguided or subconscious feelings of loyalty.

Recognizing and clearing your earliest family paradigm begins the process of releasing resistance to having more money. There's an incredible freedom when you can take all that energy and put it toward what you want to create. The most important step after recognizing your old paradigm and how it blocks you from creating a better financial situation is to use Tapping to reduce the intensity of the old emotions you discovered. Then you can make decisions based on what *you* want.

"Now I get to choose my own money paradigm and can make it one that brings me satisfaction."

When you clear something, a space is left to be filled. That's a great time to visualize what you ideally want: "This is what I want to create. This is what I want to believe." Even if you don't believe it a hundred percent yet, begin to think about what you can choose to create in your money picture. Decide to march toward this with all of your energy, as a totally different person than the one who unconsciously manifested the family's money paradigm, over and over and over. That is truly, truly a breakthrough.

Victor agreed to try Tapping after he recognized his own vows to be loyal to and rebel against the family's paradigm. He released a storehouse of anger and sadness toward his father for his painful childhood. He left feeling like a new man. Clarity about this vow filled him with understanding and empowerment, leading to a complete shift in attitude and perspective about his financial mess. It was still a huge challenge, but it no longer defined him. He reconciled with his family and returned to work to create something amazing, remembering he's a man of great vision, creativity, and know-how. Most important, he loves being that man, even without the vow against his father.

Use this script for Tapping about your family paradigm to clear all those negative blocks around it. Fill in the specific beliefs and feelings you experienced in childhood. Do it until your emotions feel neutral and calm.

TAPPING SCRIPT FOR FAMILY PARADIGM

Follow this script while Tapping through the points:

There they are—my parents *** There was panic and fear around money *** Anxiety and worry about money *** Anger and fighting about money *** Never-ending cycles of scarcity *** Of struggle, of disempowerment *** And the fear that comes with it *** We totally believed in scarcity.

(continued)

Scarcity was real in our family *** And my parents lived in it *** Fear about money *** Anger about money *** Betrayal over money! *** Hopelessness about money *** Disappointment over and over *** Disappointment about money *** And there I am, I am feeling it *** I am downloading this paradigm *** All of this programmed *** Into my subconscious mind *** Programmed into my very nervous system *** My family's money paradigm.

I honor the pain we had *** I honor the pain my parents had *** I honor the sadness, the loss, the unfairness *** And I am so open to letting this go! *** For my highest good *** Fear about money *** Depression about money *** Hopelessness and loss about money *** Shame and disappointment connected to money *** Anger and fighting connected to money *** I totally honor that was their way *** And I am open to releasing this *** So I can create my reality *** In my present moment.

Take a nice deep breath. Sometimes when you first do Tapping for this, lots of emotion is released as you connect to the loss, unfairness, and grief of your family's past. When you feel this release, you increase your consciousness of how much negative pressure related to money you carry. After Tapping, check the image of your family paradigm again. It should be calmer and feel more distant. Then identify anything vivid or loud about that scene that still feels stuck and do more specific Tapping about it. You should be able to see all the limiting beliefs your parent passed to you with more clarity. Look for and itemize your downloaded limiting beliefs about:

- How hard you have to work to deserve wealth
- The character and integrity of wealthy people
- The character and integrity of people who relax and enjoy life
- The good versus evil spirituality of wealthy people

- What happens to good people who become wealthy
- Where the line is drawn, in terms of income and savings, between you and wealthy people
- The suspicions around those who seem to get rich "easily" without backbreaking struggle
- The possibilities for empowerment, success, wealth for "people like us," in terms of social, educational, and economic class
- Whether or not it's possible to get ahead of paycheck-to-paycheck living
- What financial security looks like in terms of actual money in the bank

This exercise is critical for your consciousness, since the downloaded beliefs from your earliest money paradigm are accepted unconsciously as the undeniable truth about money, people, and the world. Once you become aware, you can clear them. Now let's get positive with an encouraging round of Tapping!

POSITIVE TAPPING FOR SHIFTING YOUR PARADIGM

Follow this script while Tapping through all the points:

I've seen something important today *** I have seen my parents' paradigm *** And it became my paradigm *** I totally honor that *** This was my parents' reality *** That came from their life *** Their beliefs, their pain *** Their paradigm! *** I never wanted this paradigm *** But I have been reliving it *** I have been loyal to it *** I have been battling it *** It has been running me.

   Now I am shining *** The light of consciousness on this *** And

(continued)

that changes everything *** I am letting go of this old paradigm *** And my vow to be loyal to it *** And my vow to re-create and battle it *** I honor my parents and all their struggles *** But this is my time now *** I want to create my own new paradigm! *** I am open to a whole new way with money *** I am open to earning much more *** Doing what I love.

I am open to feeling totally secure with money *** I am open to becoming a fantastic money manager *** I am the master of my life *** Creating my life, creating my money! *** It's my time to go further and live bigger *** And it's my choice now *** I free myself from these old rules *** I free myself from this old paradigm *** And I am now free to choose!

Do this round again until you feel the message. Positive, excited emotions generated from Tapping maintain a good vibration so you can begin to change your financial picture for the better.

Clearing the Boom and Bust Cycle in Your Money: A revealing discussion about why so many people cycle through making more money and then losing it both in their businesses or from their personal income www.TappingIntoWealth.com/Video5

6

FINANCIAL TRAUMA

Trauma comes from an event that shocks you and creates great distress or suffering, both during the event and after it's over. You might not associate this with money, but I often encounter people with these kinds of responses to their financial situation. I began to notice a distinct pattern of past traumatic stories that came up when I worked with people on their savings account (or lack thereof) or on their debt. These past events sometimes involved actual emotional or physical trauma. But even if the person didn't see the incident as traumatic, it seemed to have a strong impact—sometimes catastrophic—on the person's savings account or debt load.

Regardless of how long ago the event occurred, its negative effect could still be seen in the emotions or finances of my clients. So I felt it crucial to define this particular type of situation for what it truly is—a "financial trauma." And I want to help you identify any that you may have experienced that might be holding you back from increasing your wealth.

Identifying Trauma

Do you suffer from financial trauma? Here's the acid test for whether or not you do. Look at the numbers that represent your debt or your savings, or both. Think about them. Do any memories you regret pop up into your head: a past incident, a bad decision you made, or a person who steered you in the wrong direction? Does this elicit thoughts like, "If only this hadn't happened I'd be much further ahead" or "My financial picture would be so much better had I not done that or listened to him." If you can say that about anything you experienced in the past, you have had a financial trauma.

A financial trauma has two key elements to it. First, it's a past event that has a dramatic negative impact on your money, savings, credit, or all of them. Second, when you look at your current money situation, such as your savings account or credit score, you still see the impact of that event reflected in your numbers. Sometimes it came from a real trauma, such as an accident, betrayal, divorce, a business idea gone badly, or a catastrophic illness. Even if you've done lots of personal development or therapy work around the emotional side of what happened, you may not have dealt with how massively it affected your money. If you look at your financial picture today and still feel strong anger, sadness, or regret about a past event that greatly impacted it, then the trauma is still there. Common causes of financial trauma that I've seen are:

- Trusting someone who ripped you off
- A business gone bad
- A betrayal in a business partnership
- Having something stolen from you
- Feeling taken to the cleaners in a divorce settlement
- Making a very poor decision about an investment or business

- Not being adequately insured for a serious accident or illness
- Going into bankruptcy for any of the above reasons

If you experienced any scenario like those above, no matter how long ago, it can linger in your emotions, impact your stress level, and radically change your willingness to trust in the future. This makes it truly a financial trauma by my definition. For example, think about an event in your past that might be a financial trauma and see how true on a scale of 1 to 10 any of these statements feel:

- "Ever since that day, I don't trust myself."
- "I learned that you just can't trust other people."
- "Money brings out the dark side even in people you trust."
- "I didn't handle it well and should have known better."
- "I should've advocated for myself more."
- "The universe just totally didn't support me so I must be bad."
- "Ever since that day I'm afraid to believe and don't want to get my hopes up too high because I might be disappointed. So I don't want to try anymore."

If any of those statements feel true, you've got a financial trauma and Tapping on this will be life changing. The problem with a financial trauma is that it keeps causing pain. As you move forward in time, the memory of it goes with you, acting as irrefutable evidence of unfairness and disappointment related to money. It may even feel like in addition to the money you lost, you've lost a piece of yourself that you can never get back. Traumas in general make you feel vulnerable and unsure of yourself, suspicious of others, and worried about what can happen to you in the future. That's why people tend to avoid certain activities and experiences more after a trauma than they would have before.

Traumas in your finances cause you to avoid focusing on creating more wealth and make you skeptical about whether it's possible to change your entire wealth picture. Proof of how unfair life can be and how badly things can turn out, regardless of the amount of effort you put in, is always with you in your memories of past traumas, even when you're not conscious of them.

YOUR SAVINGS AND TRAUMA

Your savings account, or lack thereof, might be closely tied to financial trauma. When you work with income, there's always a give-and-take exchange that involves your belief in the value of your time, energy, work, intelligence, and training. With savings, there's a very different energy. As I said earlier, a savings account can represent different things to different people. It's important to see what happens when you tune in to your savings account, so do this exercise to increase your awareness.

Exercise to Identify Financial Trauma: Savings

Write down the amount in your savings right now. If you have none and/or have debt, just put the number 0. We'll deal with debt in the next chapter.

Look at that number. Then just below it, write down how much you'd love to have in your savings account. Now, I don't mean the million- or billion-dollar future vision. For now just use the number that represents the next step up from where you are now. Think in terms of how much you'd have to increase your savings account to feel more secure.

Look at those two numbers and then focus on the exact amount of savings you have. Once you've absorbed that number, say out loud, "It's not enough," "It's never been enough." Pay attention to how true that statement feels, and what emotions come up when you say it. Also see if any past events pop into your mind that contributed to your current level of savings.

The reactions that come up from the thousands of people I've worked with range from fear and panic—feelings discussed earlier in relation to survival—and also a lot of deep sadness, depression, or loss. This is a point that helps many people become more conscious of a financial trauma they may have endured. No matter how long ago it happened, the memory of a financial trauma can still trigger negative emotions and be evident in your current financial situation. Pay attention to exactly what's going on when you tune in to your savings account. It offers many clues as to why you don't have more money. To learn more, do the second part of the exercise.

Look at your savings account again, think about any related past event that still lingers in your thoughts in a negative way, and ask, "What does this mean about me?" Then look at the amount in your savings account and the gap between that and what you'd like to have, and fill in the blank: "This means I'm _____."

Once again, in addition to the strong emotions that get activated and trigger your fight-or-flight system, thinking about your savings account will also generate a different kind of very harsh talk by your inner critic. It often differs a bit from the self-talk that comes from thinking about your income in that it more specifically attacks your confidence in managing money. It will sound like:

- "I'm an idiot with money."
- "I've failed in handling my money properly."
- "I've stupidly made mistakes with my money."
- "I've made bad investments."
- "I spend too much."

Surprisingly, I've done these exercises with people who have Ph.D.s, or who are mathematicians, CPAs, accountants, and financial advisers. While they spend their entire life focused on numbers and money management for other people, they feel completely inept, inadequate, and a whole list of negative labels in their personal finances. For example, Emma was a CPA and financial adviser who earned a great living because she was fantastic at her profession. She came to work with me because she needed to do more public speaking to grow her business, but she suffered from speaking anxiety.

When working to find the root of her speaking fears, Emma revealed that she felt like a fraud as a money expert. When I asked why, she said, "Because the truth is I am a fraud. I have no savings, no security, no investments, *nada*! The real truth is that I am a terrible money manager for myself. If anyone knew that, they'd never hire me!" She was in complete panic, awake till late most nights, lamenting over her lack of financial security. And she was very angry at herself for being in that position. Though Emma made a great income, she had no savings because of a bad choice she was persuaded to make ten years earlier. This mistake still haunted her.

After her divorce, she had a nice nest egg from investing her settlement wisely. But after several years, Emma made the bold decision to invest in some property with a new boyfriend, who was very persuasive. Things appeared to be going well, and she invested even more money until all of her nest egg was gone. Suddenly everything went wrong— the boyfriend disappeared and she was left without any way to recover her losses. "If only that had not happened. If only I had not been so stupid, I'd be so much further ahead right now!" she said with the weight of the world in her words.

From that day on, it was too painful to think about rebuilding her security, given the pain and shame of the loss she'd suffered. So she didn't. We used Tapping about this old, financially traumatic event to clear all the emotional intensity and self-blame around it. Afterward, Emma was truly able to let it go emotionally. This paved the way for a huge shift in perspective about what she wanted to create in her saving and the actions she could take immediately. Emma saw how this old story and her continual self-criticism around money management held her back from owning how good she was and taking advantage of opportunities to speak. Lack of trust in herself and her avoidance of steps to rebuild her savings worked together in a vicious cycle that kept it at zero.

Once she processed it all, she was ready to create a whole new chapter in the story of her savings and security, using all of her brilliance and the knowledge she had gained working as a financial adviser. She went back to the office that night and worked until midnight to create her entire five-year financial freedom plan to the penny. She started doing what was necessary the very next day to achieve it. Within a year, she was not only speaking more to market herself, but she was also captivating audiences with her inspirational story of struggle and overcoming it to build success.

In a traumatic situation like this, you get a triple whammy. First, you have a painful emotional response that leads to negative self-talk, blaming yourself for what went wrong. This creates a loss of self-confidence, specifically in relation to how good a money manager you are in your personal life and in business. So when you have a financial trauma, wow, you have a massive upside coming once you do Tapping to clear it! As a matter of fact, Tapping is widely used as a technique to help people suffering the effects of trauma because it works so exceptionally well for releasing it.

We'll start tapping by addressing the immediate emotions that arise when you think about your lack of savings—typically fear, worry, and sadness. Then you can move on to address any financial trauma that may have played a role in negatively affecting your ability to increase your wealth.

TAPPING SCRIPT FOR LACK OF SAVINGS

Follow this script while Tapping through the points:

My savings are dismal *** It's depressing *** It fills me with anxiety *** So I try not to think about it *** I don't want to think about it *** And it reminds me *** How different things could have been.

It feels like I have lost so much *** Feeling safe and supported *** So very sad *** Maybe I have never really felt safe *** No security *** What if something happens? *** I have no safety net *** Disappointment and sadness *** It feels like loss *** I am feeling it *** Sad and unsafe *** All because of my *lack* of savings.

Sadness and fear welling up in me *** I should be so much further ahead *** It feels impossible! *** But I honor my feelings *** And my true desire *** To be safe and supported.

Notice how the emotions can tend to get more intense before they start to lighten up.

Try tapping through the script again until the words feel less charged and don't feel very true. Now tune in to any past story that fits the description of a financial trauma affecting your current level of savings. First, measure on a scale of 1 to 10 how intense you feel when you think about that event and write down the feelings and the intensity (1 being none and 10 being the worst).

TAPPING SCRIPT FOR A FINANCIAL TRAUMA THAT AFFECTED SAVINGS

Follow this script while Tapping through the points:

I know exactly why I have so little saved *** It all started in that past story *** I can see it all so clearly *** So I try not to think about it *** But the evidence is loud and clear *** I am still paying the price of that day *** How different things could have been! *** If only I hadn't made those choices.

If that hadn't happened *** Looking back it is so frustrating *** And so unfair *** I wish I could change it! *** But I can't and that's depressing *** Demoralizing! *** And the mistakes I made *** Why was I so stupid?

And the betrayal of it all *** Such a shock *** I am still shocked *** It destroyed my finances *** And it's hard to let that go *** Why should I? *** No one understands the trouble it caused *** And how much money I lost.

How can I forgive and forget? *** I honor this story and all my feelings *** I am open to letting this go *** So I can start with a whole new energy *** I could start today *** If I can let go of this story *** I can be free to start over!

Now take a breath and recheck how intense you feel when you think about that story again. Tapping will continue to neutralize the emotions and memories of the event so you can move on with the energy to start anew. It's important to make the connection that every time you think about the amount in your savings account, it triggers an entire fight-or-flight response in your body—fear, anxiety, panic, frustration, and negative emotions like sadness, depression, loss, as well as very harsh inner talk, and shame focused on your ability or inability as a money manager.

Ask yourself, "How much time would I be willing to spend totally focused on setting and achieving a goal for my savings account?" I mean totally focused on all the action, energy, and attention needed to double or triple your savings account, or even increase it by tenfold or a hundredfold. Many people don't do this or even consider it because it brings up bad feelings, as it did for Emma. People want a healthy savings account, but have no goal or plan, and take no action. Facing the reality of your savings, or lack of it, can be depressing. This is where Tapping is an especially powerful tool to reduce, turn off, and clear all this heavy emotional baggage that comes up when you think about your savings account.

Tapping can completely change your focus, enthusiasm, and beliefs by releasing the story of a financial trauma connected to your savings. It can also stoke your willingness to set goals for saving more and pursue them in a more effective way. This has the power to make a positive difference. After doing some rounds on it, you may actually be excited and energized about building your account and even enthusiastically think, "This is where I am now and I so want to greatly increase my money!" That's when things start to change and shift.

When you build renewed excitement and focus, you can make the commitment to becoming a fantastic money manager. This is important because earning is only half the picture. To grow your savings quickly, you'll need solid money management skills and strategies. When you've got lots of negative emotion affecting your actions, you won't put the time, energy, and focus into being an empowered money manager. You could take a million classes, read books on how to do it, and set better goals. But until you clear any financial trauma you have, you won't be able to use the lessons effectively.

TAPPING SCRIPT FOR CREATING FABULOUS SAVINGS

Follow this script while Tapping through the points:

When I look at my savings account *** And remember that old story *** I often criticize myself *** And question my money savvy *** I am not really a great money manager *** I sometimes feel inept with my finances *** Or maybe I have *never* been smart with money *** And I often review all the evidence I have that reinforces that I am bad with money *** A criticism and a foregone conclusion *** No wonder I don't put a lot of focus on money management *** No wonder I don't have a plan *** Well, that was then, and this is now *** I may not have all the skills I need today *** But I now commit to growing myself *** Into a much better money manager!

I am smart *** I can learn *** And now I am open to putting in the time *** I am open to focusing on my finances *** And becoming a smart and savvy money manager *** Maybe even a million-dollar money manager *** And as I focus on my savings account *** It will grow and expand *** I can learn from the past *** And grow into my future *** I *can* do this *** And I am starting today!

If you're now aware of a financial trauma that impacts you and your finances and it still feels very intense, use Tapping more specifically by simply Tapping while telling the story of what happened. As different thoughts and emotions arise, voice them loudly. Sometimes you can get stuck on the story when the things that happened seemed very unfair and still feel unresolved, like "No one admitted that he or she was wrong or apologized," or "I never got compensated or even validated for my loss." In that case, you'll have more resistance to letting it go, unless you allow yourself to voice the trauma, even if it sounds a bit like you're complaining or crying "poor me." Tapping allows this stuck trauma to clear and become less important to you and your life today. You can also try what I call the movie technique, which is described in chapter 11.

Using Tapping on a financial trauma is one of the most powerfully enlightening and freeing things you can do. Financial trauma messes with the energy and vibe around your money in a huge way. Every time you look at how little you have, you may remember that trauma and then all the emotional baggage filters in. You may not realize it on a conscious level but your body will feel it and the Law of Attraction will respond to it. Every time you look at your money situation, think about that event, and feel negative emotions, it hinders your ability to follow through on statements like "I will be an empowered money manager," "I will double my business," "I will make it happen this time." Good intentions get thwarted by financial trauma.

You can say those affirmations all day long but they won't stick if your internal dialogue says, "I screwed up," "I didn't do it right," "I didn't learn my lesson and now don't trust myself." Humans are wired to be confident. When something happens that makes you stop trusting yourself, other people, or the universe, you withdraw from taking steps to better yourself instead of expanding into a person who can increase your wealth. Traumatic events can keep you contracted, afraid, tight, and guarded around money. Nothing you do that's related to money will be the same while you come from that place of trauma.

When you use Tapping to clear the energy, memory, and negative emotions tied to your trauma, you'll have an amazing upside and gift coming. The boost to your overall energy, attitude, enthusiasm, and especially your self-confidence is hard to describe because it can be so great.

Let's Have Fun with Tapping for $50,000: A great way of Tapping that will leave you excited, energized, and feeling great about money
www.TappingIntoWealth.com/Video6

7

HOW DEBT KEEPS
YOU STUCK

Have you ever noticed how awful the word "debt" can make you feel? When you have some form of bad debt, like money owed on a credit card or a debt consolidation loan, there can be a feeling about it that looms in your mind and creates negative emotions like a dark cloud. Some even describe that feeling as "agony," because it's always there, always negative. And the more you think about any debt you have, the worse you usually feel! That's why people tend to avoid thinking about it.

Emotional Debt

There are two main kinds of debt—good and bad. Good debt includes assets and investments that grow in value and/or are leveraged to create income. A home mortgage is an example of good debt, since your payments create an asset you'll own instead of just paying rent with no equity from it. While some people have homes that are worth less than they paid, most are an investment that grows in value. Although good debt does mean a bill to pay, it doesn't create the same negative feelings that bad debt does. It's actually quite the opposite, since good debt shows that you've invested well and are building and leveraging your money wisely.

It's important to understand where bad debt comes from because its source, or how it was created, will greatly affect how you feel about it. Most credit card debt comes from purchasing things that get used up or decrease in value, like clothes, dinners, or stuff bought impulsively. Debt loans can result from consolidating credit cards or something worse. It can be caused by a financial trauma like medical bills after an illness or accident, or from a business that went south, or a personal betrayal.

Bad debt, which is the focus of this chapter, can cause panic, or the feeling of being overwhelmed or sick to your stomach. Having bad debt is like a black hole that pulls your good intentions about creating wealth down into a spiral of negativity. That may sound a bit over the top until you look hard at all the negative impacts of owing money. From the perspective of the Law of Attraction, it truly is a negative spiral. Once you accrue some debt, your situation can get even worse because of the thoughts that the Law of Attraction picks up and returns to you.

Here's how it works. Thoughts about debt invade your mind, keeping some level of panic in your present reality. That causes worry about the future and thoughts of everything you won't get to do. You may wonder how you'll pay it off, or whether it will get worse, leading to trouble falling asleep or waking during the night in a panic. Debt triggers the stress response for millions of people multiple times every day. Since the Law of Attraction brings more of what you think about, constant strong emotions like panic and worry about debt means you'll attract what you do *not* want more of. This makes it very difficult to use the Law of Attraction effectively, since those negative emotions will override any positive vision.

While it's counterproductive, focusing *a lot* on your debt and worrying about it can seem like the responsible thing to do. It's as though there's a belief that it's productive, or part of the "I need to learn my lesson" or self-punishment process to keep it in the forefront of your mind. But when that gets overwhelming and demoralizing, the tendency is to shift gears and try to pretend it's not there. Unfortunately, the worry and anxiety are always there on some level, omnipresent just below the surface of consciousness and keeping you in a negative state.

Financial debt causes a pile of negative emotions—anger, frustration, hopelessness, helplessness, and/or guilt directed at yourself, the world, creditors, the government, your partner, and so on. Most people who feel tremendous guilt and embarrassment about their debt also believe they deserve to feel that way, since they created it. It can lead to feeling like a victim. No good comes from both having all these negative emotions *and* believing that you deserve it as a sort of punishment for your debt. That just makes you feel lower about yourself, your abilities, and your potential. Carrying around those feelings robs you of the very energy, vision, and creativity needed to get out of debt.

~ *Worrying about debt creates more debt.* ~

Since thoughts of your debt can replay over and over, you can experience this extremely negative place often. It can be agony, often leading people to a favorite way to neutralize emotional pain—spending more money! We jokingly call it "retail therapy." It can help you feel good for a short time but escalates the debt that causes the pain. Buying new, pretty, fun things gives you a mini-boost and escape. But it worsens debt problems when the bills come. And there are many other unhealthy therapies to drown the pain of debt, which I think of as "overs"—overeating, overdrinking, and overpartying. These drain money and leave you feeling worse after the rush fades.

DEBT AND YOUR INNER WORTH

Is there a deeper meaning in your debt? When you look at something like the dollars-and-cents total of your debt, it can be very difficult to recognize that this can be changed by using personal development work and a technique like Tapping. Debt appears as a real and immediate problem caused by external circumstances and sometimes your mistakes. It doesn't seem like a calling to look within. I admit, I found it hard to make the connection when I first heard financial expert Suze Orman say, "Your inner worth is manifested in your net worth." But if you're willing to look further, you'll see that your debt absolutely requires inner work to resolve it.

Regardless of how you got into debt and what achievements you've made in other areas of your life, debt is always a reminder that you're falling short. It reflects that what you do to earn money, when measured in dollars and cents, is not enough. Debt says that the value of your gifts, time, and energy is just not enough. This is often exactly what people say about their debt: "I feel like no matter how hard I work, no matter what I do, it's never enough." When you're able to look at debt as the result of an inner belief, you can begin to understand that it's a manifestation of something deep inside that says, on some level, you don't have enough value; that your gifts, talents, hard work, and time aren't valuable enough to get the kind of wealth you'd like.

~ *Debt is a measurable, black-and-white, dollars-and-cents,*
real-world reflection of your inner worth. ~

To identify on what level this inner belief holds you back, look at the balance in your life between your effort/hours/energy and income. Countless numbers of people work long hours with passion, helping others, and sacrificing for their jobs. Many *appear* to be very successful. They're loved and respected for their tireless commitment to the people they work with or help. Yet they have a dirty little secret of being in debt, which rules how they feel inside, despite their outward appearance. This is their way of manifesting, in indisputable dollars and cents, their real secret—an inner competing belief about not being good enough. Debt reflects what you believe, often subconsciously, about your worth in a material, measurable form. If you have it, look deeper at your innermost beliefs about your worth and how you evaluate the value of your time and energy. That's a good step for increasing wealth.

While some of this may sound dismal, when you do the necessary work on your inner beliefs, you'll no longer need to manifest debt and you'll stop your pattern of getting into situations where you end up owing money. By ridding yourself of those inner beliefs and increasing your self-worth (more in chapter 12), your debt will dissolve with it. How does that happen? Remember, your inner world generates the creativity, energy, and actions that form your outer world. When you increase your inner belief in your value and worth, all the ways you earn and manage your money will shift to reflect that higher value!

Identifying How Debt Makes You Feel

You can approach the emotions behind your debt step by step with Tapping. If you focus on reducing and eliminating all of the negative reactions to debt, you can free yourself from old beliefs and emotions that keep you in debt. Even if you currently don't owe any money, try a few rounds anyway and see how you feel. Oftentimes, people without any debt have a lot of fear and worry about going into debt in the future. Here's an exercise to test your emotions concerning debt, broken into two parts. Here's the first one:

Exercise for Feelings about Debt #1

On a piece of paper, write down the total amount of your debt in very large numerals with a big dollar sign in front of the number. Some people use red marker, since visually it triggers more emotions. Be brutally honest with yourself and add up everything you owe from credit cards to personal loans or car loans. You may feel like you always struggle to make ends meet, even if you're earning a decent income. This can mean you've been lying to yourself and living beyond your means, which only increases debt levels.

Facing this debt number is hard for most people, but it will give you a new sense of power and bolster your determination to eliminate that debt. Look at that number and say the following out loud with your number inserted: "I have five thousand dollars in debt," "I have fifty thousand dollars in debt." As you say it, pay attention to feelings and raw sensations that arise when you speak that number.

Your emotions will typically appear very quickly when you think about, talk about, and tune in to your debt. As discussed in chapter 5, these are emotions that you're programmed from childhood to experience when you deal with or think about money. Ninety-nine percent of the time, the emotion you feel first when looking at your debt is the primary one that drives how you operate in relation to money. If anxiety and fear come up, which is common, recognize that and take a moment to absorb it to give yourself personal clarity and consciousness: "I am programmed to operate in fear around money. I am programmed to operate in panic around money." People come up with a host of feelings in addition to that first emotion, ranging from fear to anxiety to panic, and feeling sadness about them all.

It's vital to understand that this is more than just saying, "Wow, I feel anxious when I look at my debt." Your money anxiety affects how you operate with regard to money all the time. It's not just about what you owe. It affects many aspects of how you handle money and the level of wealth you can achieve. When you clear these feelings, you'll notice a big shift in several monetary areas. Now that you've identified some feelings that your debt evokes, try the second part of this exercise to understand how your debt makes you see yourself.

Exercise for Feelings about Debt #2

Think about your debt and then finish this sentence: "This debt means I'm _____."

Once you've identified what your primary operating emotion is, what you put into the second blank shows how you connect money to your feelings of self-worth and personal power. Typically, people fill in this blank with some pretty dark stuff. The most common way people answer is, "This means I am a loser. The number is right there on paper. There's nothing else it could mean." When you determine who you are through the filter of emotions created by having debt, you can be very hard on yourself. For example, other common things people fill in the blank with are:

- "This means that no matter what I do, it's never enough."
- "This means I'm hopeless. I'm helpless. I'm powerless."
- "This means I'm not smart enough to get wealthy."
- "This means the Law of Attraction doesn't work for me."

These feelings are part of how you define yourself and your power, and reveal how debt skews your self-image. When you reflect on your debt this way, how you fill in the blanks in these two sentences may be devastating. As I said in chapter 3, often the darkest, most negative stuff that people experience comes up when they think about how having debt makes them feel. That happened to Marie, an attorney who together with her husband made a great income. She came to work with me because they lived in panic and strife over their checking account and paying the bills. They were constantly overdrawn, bills piled up and were paid late, and they had yet to set up any college fund for their sons or retirement plans for themselves.

Though in general they were a close and happy couple, dealing with the bills and their balances was painful because they oscillated between total silence and avoidance, to blame and frustrated arguing. Marie knew they were on a disastrous path and wanted so much to manage their finances better, but in this one area of her life, she felt terrified and incompetent. As we explored her reactions, she revealed, "I can't complain because I caused all this. I saddled my husband and whole family with all this debt." She was filled with a sense of utter helplessness and despair because, as she said, "That is just our reality and we can never get out from under this!"

All this self-blame and guilt kept Marie immobilized from taking any proactive role in their bills and prevented her and her husband from ever having a real discussion about their goals for retirement and college funds. "What would be the point?" she asked. After Tapping to clear all this guilt about causing the debt, Marie had a massive shift in her outlook. Suddenly the smart and savvy attorney in her appeared ready for action and victory. She found the courage and willingness to sit down with her husband to really look at their finances and lay out an action plan that represented progress toward the future. Her husband went from total resistance to feeling relieved and supported, particularly when he watched her run to the mailbox with glee to pay the bills on time.

Clearing the Need for Debt

If you feel resistant to doing the above exercise or if you're overcome by negative emotions when you fill in the blanks, I encourage you to work through it because the Tapping can allow you to move out of this uncomfortable place very quickly and make you feel safer. Freeing yourself from this uncomfortable place gives you the ability to make new choices about your power that allow you to move from debt to wealth, its polar opposite.

Sometimes these exercises trigger memories of past situations or events that created your debt, along with the anger, hurt, regret, and/or sadness that still linger. If new feelings come up, it means you've identified something very important! This is a financial trauma connected to your debt. As I said in chapter 6, financial trauma is often involved in the debt of clients and people who attend my workshops.

Preparing for the first Tapping exercise can take a little time. Reflect back on the emotions you identified in first exercise about how your debt makes you feel. Look at your debt number and how you answered: "This means I'm _____." The first Tapping exercise refers to negative thoughts that most people report. I include some very dark emotions. Substitute your own words when possible. Remember that when you Tap on very dark thoughts as if they're true, you don't reinforce them. True or not, Tapping will dissipate them.

TAPPING SCRIPT FOR FEELINGS
ABOUT DEBT #1

Tap through the points, using the following phrases or your own:

I have all this debt *** And I am feeling it *** I feel anxiety *** It feels like life and death *** This is really bad; I feel panic, fear, and worry *** And I'm so ashamed, so embarrassed *** And I should be ashamed; I judge that I deserve shame *** It is really unforgivable *** That is how it feels.

My debt is shameful and embarrassing *** And it means I'm _____ *** Ooh, that hurts; wow, that's harsh; this means I'm losing *** I'm a failure *** What I do is never enough *** And I really feel that right in my stomach *** This means I probably deserve it.

The sadness, the fear *** The disappointment, the powerlessness *** I really feel the loss in this debt *** I never get to feel safe because of this debt *** I never get to feel solid ground in my money *** All this emotion in this debt *** I totally honor it.

Now take a nice deep breath. Repeat this round again. The first round takes the edge off these emotions, but when debt is a serious issue, it will take more than one round to bring down some of those emotions. Modify your words to match what you feel most strongly. This next round focuses on the feelings and beliefs that what you do is never enough. Be honest—on a scale of 1 to 10, how true is the following statement? "Whatever I do, it's just not enough—it's never enough."

That can help you gauge your feelings in this Tapping round.

TAPPING SCRIPT FOR FEELINGS
ABOUT DEBT #2

Say the following phrases aloud while Tapping on the karate chop point:

Even though I hate looking at my debt, it reminds me that whatever I do, it's just not enough and it feels like I can never win.

Continue Tapping through all the points, using the following phrases:

I hate this *** I can never win *** Never get a break *** Whatever I do is never enough *** Maybe I'm not enough *** This makes me feel so powerless *** Whatever I do is not enough *** It feels like I'm just not enough.

    I mustn't be, because I keep falling short *** I mustn't be enough *** There it is as proof for me in black and white *** In dollars and cents, my debt shows I'm not enough *** I just can't make it work *** I mustn't be doing it right *** I'm just not enough *** This old belief and programming that tells me I'm just not enough *** What I do is just not enough.

Take a nice deep breath. Measure how you feel right now. This round can bring up a lot of feelings, emotions, thoughts, memories, or physical sensations. Write them down. Each issue is "Tappable." As you conquer them, it can help you to break out of your past patterns. The first two rounds of Tapping will shift you into feeling neutral about debt. People often report feeling calmer, saying things like, "This is just how it is right now. I'm looking at a number but it doesn't make me feel like a failure. It's just a number on paper." That's a huge shift out of the fight-or-flight response of fear, anger, and sadness. And it helps you let go of the negative self-image you identified above.

The next Tapping exercise will intentionally raise your good vibe by helping you remember good things about yourself and declaring some positive statements. Once you've gotten your negative emotions cleared with the first Tapping exercise, it's time to declare to yourself and the world, "I really do want to repay this debt. I'm a person of integrity. I have pride and feel good about that. I'm now open to being supported in this goal, in this intention." When you think about your debt before negative emotions are cleared, you seldom say the word "yes" to anything related to it. It's easier just to try to avoid it. You don't honor yourself for your desire to pay it off or to change.

There's a big difference when you shift from the dark side to a more positive one, which truly is a game changer. Once you've gotten to a more neutral place, everything changes because you change—from feelings like anger, sadness, and shame to feelings of hope, enthusiasm, confidence, and honor. Then your whole vibration for manifesting money gets stronger. This next Tapping exercise begins that process.

TAPPING SCRIPT FOR SAYING "YES" TO ELIMINATING DEBT

Tap through the points, using the following phrases or your own:

There it is *** It is still my debt *** It hasn't changed *** But somehow I have changed, I feel calmer *** I see this debt as simply my present reality, and that can change *** I feel more open to the possibility and it is my intention *** To deal with this, to clear this debt. That's a *very* good intention *** I am a person of integrity—and I honor myself for that *** The truth is, I would love to clear this debt quickly *** I've been beating myself up for having it *** I've been torturing myself for having it *** A lot of energy that I've been using *** That I would love to put toward this debt *** In a positive way because I really want to repay this *** And that is the truth *** It is honorable so I honor myself right now! *** So now I am clear and it's time for me to say *Yes*.

Yes to new ideas, resources, and support *** Yes to action, learning, and growth that can speed my debt repayment *** I've been telling myself I do not deserve that *** And I am now realizing that's been keeping me down *** I'm actually open to miracles right now showing up to help me *** I'm open to miracles in myself *** Ideas, actions, persistence *** I've learned enough lessons from my debt *** I'm ready to let it go *** I'm ready to let go of the energy of it *** The sadness of it *** The powerlessness of it *** And I'm ready to say yes *** To everything I need *** To let it come quickly ***I'm saying yes to miracles *** A miracle of repayment! *** And I am saying *yes* to me *** Because I *can* do it!

Take a nice deep breath. Allow yourself a moment to write down any inspirations that come to mind as you complete this positive Tapping. Notice how differently you feel when you think about your debt now. When your blocks are removed, inspiration can flow in quickly and unexpectedly, leaving you a lot more receptive to having a better financial picture.

MOVING FROM DEBT TO WEALTH

The words "wealth" and "money" are often used interchangeably, but wealth represents much more. It can be defined as money you've amassed in ways that make you feel safe, secure, and supported, allowing you to feel like you have more freedom. For many people, this is a savings account with several months of living expenses covered. Or it can be any assets that allow you to feel like you have more freedom financially. It's the opposite of debt, which makes you afraid, unsafe, stuck, and disempowered. Wealth results from your inner program and two very important outer factors. The first is obviously *your income*, which affects how much you have, since wealth is money you've amassed. The second factor that determines the extent of wealth is *money management*.

In order to have wealth, you need both income and money management activities. The formula to amass wealth is simple: start with your income and add money management activities. A case in point is the many immigrants who come to the United States, work for years at a basic wage, and manage their income wisely. Despite not having a big income, they save enough to send their kids to college and to retire. Then there are people who earn hundreds of thousands of dollars but spend every cent and have no wealth. You need both income and money management for that income. This factor is often overlooked in Law of Attraction work.

When I say this in a workshop, someone almost always asks, "Why do people struggle with money management activities if it's simple?" The answer is that people let their emotions unconsciously run their money behavior. They buy things impulsively, or make financial decisions that don't serve them. Many people say very plainly, "I'm a bad money manager!" That reinforces their inability to manage their money and prevents them from accumulating wealth. Good money management starts with focusing your attention and brilliance on how you deal with money as well as your true wealth and income goals. When you're enthusiastic about it, you'll recognize when you don't have a strategy and find smarter ones that work for you.

I'm often asked, "Don't people with debt just need to budget better?" Managing money and setting and achieving wealth goals often include budgeting. This works best when it's part of a plan to reach a bigger, positive goal, especially one that brings you closer to achieving what you really want and are excited about. Your attitude about budgeting will make or break your chance for it being successful. Unfortunately, most budgets feel like punishment if you have to squeeze all the fun and freedom from your life to adjust to spending less money. Then budgeting feels like scarcity and often fails. After a while you'll rebel and abandon it.

But there's an upside. When you approach creating a budget correctly, it will feel less like withholding spending and more like reaching for your goal or working on your wealth plan. Focusing on your goal makes it easier to curb impulse spending consciously, from a place of power, not scarcity. You can say things like, "I'm not buying that today because I'm more excited about this goal I've set," instead of "I can't get that because I can't afford it." Managing and keeping more of your money gives you a better chance to create the wealth you envision.

> ~ *Budgeting to scarcity reinforces scarcity.*
> *Budgeting to a goal reinforces the goal.* ~

There are key steps to make the transition from debt to wealth. First, get to a point where money management becomes second nature and you do it automatically. This is hard. Tapping will help clear some of your emotions about debt and make it much easier to develop great money management strategies. But it's also necessary to start creating more income. In order to transition from debt to wealth, you need to:

- **Identify and clear away the negative emotions you've been programmed to feel around money.** Whether you have debt or your feelings about money come from other sources, uncover those emotions and clear them.

- **Seriously decide to change your money management activities.** Examine how you act in regards to money, and work to meet goals you set in order to transform debt into wealth. Then take conscious action that leads to true progress. Visualizing more money doesn't count as action. Change how you actually handle money on a day-to-day basis. Handle actual money in your hands.
- **Increase your income.** The fastest way to grow your income is to take a big step up in your mission, your personal power, and the way that you give your gifts to the world. Leave yourself open to all the possibilities for increasing your bottom line. Once you take the other steps, you'll be much more open to money opportunities.

TAPPING ON MONEY MANAGEMENT

Tapping on money management can clear some of the barriers you may have about taking charge of your money. I included some in the last chapter, but it's so important that I address more here. Although it may not seem sexy or exciting, it's a critical part of the equation to repay debts and become wealthier. The next round of Tapping will voice your commitment to a new way of dealing with money on a day-to-day basis. This is an important commitment because many people say, "I'm really bad with money," not realizing that the universe is listening. The more you say things like that, the more it becomes reality. When you Tap, be open to making a commitment to being a fabulous, empowered money manager.

TAPPING SCRIPT FOR COMMITTING
TO BEING A MONEY MANAGER

Say the following phrases aloud while Tapping on the karate chop point:

Even though the truth is I've manifested this debt, which means I haven't managed my money well, I totally honor myself anyway. I'm committing right now to being a better money manager.

Even though the truth is I avoid money, I do not manage it well, I've never had a clear plan, and I have bad habits, I totally honor myself. And this is my time now! This is the time for the entire planet now to make a new choice to manage money well.

Continue Tapping through all the points using the following phrases:

I commit to shifting myself *** From fear and bad habits, to a whole new way of dealing with money *** I am totally open to a whole new way *** That works perfectly for me *** Not somebody else's way *** A way that feels good for me *** I love the idea of managing lots of money *** So I'm letting the universe know.

I'm not sure I'm a great money manager today *** But I now commit *** To growing myself *** Into a fabulous money manager *** I do not know how to do it today *** But I have faith the universe will deliver to me *** Everything I need to learn this new skill, and I'm ready for it to be fun *** I commit to being an empowered money manager *** Heck, yeah!

Take a nice deep breath. This Tapping exercise should drive home that it's your day-to-day dealings with money that make the difference between debt and wealth, no matter what your income is. People often wonder how to practice money management if they're in debt and have no money to manage. Tapping is a critical step to eliminating debt and beginning your journey toward financial independence because this journey has to start somewhere. Debt transformation does not truly begin until you take the time to plan your actions and commit to changing your money habits. Tapping will help you commit and stick to a debt reduction strategy.

The Quantum Leap from Debt to REAL Wealth: Knocking out all your resistance to creating REAL wealth with an outrageous way of Tapping www.TappingIntoWealth.com/Video7

8

YOUR HIDDEN AGENDAS

I n the next two chapters, you'll take steps to move forward to a new
wealth reality by creating larger goals that both motivate and inspire your ideas and actions. But first there's very important work
to do. You need to uncover and clear any secret agenda that may be
attached to making much more money. This is made up of the many
things you've connected to and projected onto making more money—
underlying reasons for reaching your goals. If left in place, this agenda
can distract, delay, and derail the energy, focus, and action that should
be directed at your goal. How do you find your secret agenda? Here's
an exercise to reveal all facets of it.

Understanding Your Hidden Agenda

Exercise for Finding Your Hidden Agenda

In the next chapter, you'll set an income goal, but for now, pick an income goal number for this exercise that's three to four times bigger than your current one. Imagine yourself earning at that level in the future and answer these questions:

When I'm earning that much, I'll finally feel:

1._____, 2._____, 3._____

I'll finally know that I'm:

1._____, 2._____, 3._____

I'll have finally proved to [NAME] that I'm _____.

Some examples of what I commonly hear are:

- "I'll finally feel safe!"
- "I'll finally feel peaceful, joyful, powerful."
- "I'll finally feel validated and know I'm smart enough, good enough, a winner."
- "I'll finally know that I'm good enough to make a good income."
- "I'll finally prove to my mother/father/teachers that I can do it, that I chose the right path, and can do it my own way and succeed."
- "I'll finally prove to everyone that they were wrong about me. I am special."

For some, there's also proof of more universal and spiritual truths:

- God does care about/reward good people, God does care about me
- The Law of Attraction/believing against all odds does really work
- The universe really is abundant; dreams do come true

These motives represent a secret little agenda of personal and emotional needs that we attach to our income goal. They can be categorized into three buckets:

1. Things you'll finally get to feel—like safe or free
2. Things you'll finally get to prove or have validated—like your worth or brilliance
3. A person you'll finally get to be—a winner, powerful, respected

What's revealed in your answers is an entire agenda of emotional and psychological needs that you've unconsciously attached to earning more money. This agenda puts an additional level of pressure on you and adds meaning that shouldn't be part of your goal for more money. In many cases, this meaning comes from a lifelong inner battle with yourself, your parents, the naysayers, or God.

HOW HIDDEN AGENDAS BLOCK GOALS
Instead of having freedom to grow your income through the joy of giving your talents, gifts, or valuable products/service to many more people, any hidden agenda that's woven into your goal creates emotional havoc as you move toward it. Have you ever worked on a project or on a team with someone who had a hidden agenda? You get the clear sense

that the goal on paper is way less important to them than something they don't acknowledge. Surprisingly, those with hidden agendas are often the saboteurs of the goal. That's why it's so important to see and clear any that are attached to yours before you get started.

If you don't clear your underlying agenda, it will create bigger/ unrealistic expectations and more devastating lows as you work toward goals. When you encounter normal challenges, underlying agendas make them feel much more personal. Instead of seeing your goal as being delayed or challenged by something you can work through and overcome, it may feel like the need tied to your hidden agenda is being withheld or thwarted. So you'll become more frustrated, disappointed, sad, anxious, even depressed, with less energy and focus to rise to the challenge.

Consultants often experience this. They can handle any challenge for someone else's project or goal with positive focus and enthusiasm, but are much more emotionally reactive and drained by challenges in their own business. Think back on goals you've set for yourself and how you reacted to challenges. If you look hard, you may recognize that something lying beneath ran the show and battled with your goals. For example, when you attach an agenda like, "When I get there I'll finally be validated as good enough, worthy, etc.," it means you've had a life-long cycle of not feeling validated.

You may subconsciously view this as if you're battling to overcome or disprove a "truth" you've believed: "I'll never be smart enough." When you're in this battle, there's always a cycle that plays out over and over with different people and different circumstances. For this example, the cycle could go like this:

- You have an unconscious but habitual way of operating to prove you're good enough, smart enough, worthy, or the like in order to earn validation.

- You attract people who match the battle—critical, negative, and difficult to please—and who often reinforce that "You're not good enough."
- You attract circumstances and situations that seem to prove that you've missed something, made mistakes, or haven't done enough.
- You then battle against the people and circumstances but end up feeling hurt, devastated, disappointed, and even disempowered.
- When you recover, you restart the cycle in an endeavor that seems completely new on the surface, with a new cast of characters, but it's the same script.

This cycle may have played out many times in your past. It can be incredibly enlightening and empowering to take a step back and see the pattern from this viewpoint. If you bring your hidden agenda unconsciously into your income goal, you'll attract the people and conditions that play out this cycle of battle and sabotage your efforts.

The truth is, your personal needs for security, freedom, and validation of your worth, choices, and brilliance are real and should be acknowledged honestly. Becoming more conscious of them allows you to take action to meet these real needs and remove them from the secret agenda list. When you deal with them, you free yourself to work on your income goals for the joy of creating something amazing, rather than trying to prove something.

IDENTIFYING YOUR HIDDEN AGENDAS
Here's a map of sorts—examples to further guide you in finding any hidden agendas you've played out in the past. You'll play them out again unless you become conscious of them and change the pattern.

Example #1: "I need to earn this money. When I do, I'll finally feel safe and secure." This comes from a history of never feeling that way. It's reflected in your money and other areas of your life. The battle is against a belief that you'll never be safe or have enough money to support yourself, the belief that people in general are not to be trusted. Anxiety about finances, goals, and relationships creates cycles of overworking or being stuck in fear. You attract people and situations that reinforce those fears. As the cycle progresses, you'll feel more sadness, anxiety, and disillusionment, unless you clear the underlying agenda.

Example #2: "I need to earn this money. Then I'll finally feel validated and prove I'm good enough, smart enough, worthy." This comes from a history of never feeling completely seen, rewarded, and validated for your talents. You battle against past experiences with people who indicate you're not good enough, and you fear being exposed as failing, wrong, not good enough, and the like. The cycle is designed to achieve the validation you crave. Nonetheless, you'll attract people and situations that reinforce "I'm not good enough yet." As it progresses, you'll feel more self-critical, depressed, frustrated, disempowered, with lower self-esteem and confidence.

Example #3: "I need to earn this money. When I do, I'll prove I was right and they (parents, teachers, siblings, etc.) were wrong about me and what I can accomplish." This comes from a history of always feeling that others put you down, never believing in you or trying to squash your dreams. The battle is against experiencing situations and people that made you feel like a failure—that you'll never amount to anything and will always mess up. The cycle operates in boom and bust mode, creating amazing wins, and then sabotaging everything. You'll attract people and situations that reinforce the idea that "The world is in battle against me and my worth. Maybe I am a loser." As the cycle progresses, you'll feel anger, rage, brokenness, and depression.

I found a secret agenda in Patrick, a businessman, father, and husband. As a child, his father verbally abused him and his family, and drank away all their money. Patrick's mother was always worried and scared, since she barely had enough to feed her children. He vividly remembered swearing to never be anything like his father and hated him. Patrick was determined to be a good father and *never* experience that kind of lack again. As he built a successful business and became a family man, his father and his vow stayed in his thoughts. Although his father had passed away years before, Patrick spoke to him in his head as he became wealthy and successful: "See! I said I'd never be like you!" he railed at the sky, "You said I'd always fail, but I've won, Dad. I'm nothing like you!"

Then everything started to collapse. Within eighteen months from the peak of his success, Patrick lost the majority of his business and money. His wife had to work longer hours. He oscillated between total disbelief, being frozen with panic, and feeling angry and betrayed by everyone, including God. Patrick was ashamed of not being able to provide financially for his family and became depressed. He eventually moved out, since it was too painful to see his wife work so hard. Patrick admitted to me, "I've become everything I hate and swore never to be. I'm just like my father." He had re-created, through people and situations, the pattern he'd battled against his whole life. I worked with Patrick to clear his immediate guilt, shame, and anger about his situation.

Afterward, he could see his battle cycle clearly and the way he attached a secret agenda of "proving his father wrong" to every achievement. His successes always spiraled to ruin through his own unconscious self-sabotage, so the battle cycle could repeat. This understanding changed Patrick instantly! As his huge weight lifted, he was suddenly freed from old chains and began to rebuild his life and fortune with soaring energy, confidence, and determination. He was then able to reconcile with his family and start setting new wealth and business goals for the joy of creating life his way, not to prove his father wrong.

DIRECTING YOUR AGENDAS TO THE POSITIVE

What should be your deeper driving force behind simply achieving a sum of money? This is an important question because it's where you find your bigger charge of motivation and clarity. Working toward your goal should be rewarding and enjoyable. That's a good agenda! A huge income increase usually creates a noticeable difference in your lifestyle in general that's fun and exciting. A second good agenda is that increased income will always come through giving more of your valuable products, service, and/or talents to a greater number of people. Imagine doing what you love most and giving your best to many more people who are thrilled to benefit from what you offer.

If you triple your income, it means you're also tripling the amount of unique value you put out. Notice when you give what you love most and are uniquely best at, you feel the most alive, enthusiastic, passionate, and energized and can see your value as it's received by others. When you remember these two motivations and put them squarely in your consciousness, you attach a motivation to your goal that's for your highest and truest good, as well as the good of everyone you receive money from. You're free to want to earn this money because you'll love giving your gift and being more "you" every day. When challenges to the goal come along, your attitude, energy, focus, and brilliance will rise to the occasion! So how do you start shifting this to the right agenda? Do this exercise:

Exercise for Directing Your Hidden Agenda

Get very clear and honest about hidden agendas in your goals by completing the sentences you did earlier: "I really need this money because then I will finally be_____, prove _____, feel_____."

Then make a very honest admission that sounds something like this: "The truth is, I've attached my lifelong need to feel validated, smart enough, good enough to my income goal like a secret hidden agenda. This keeps me in a cycle of battling with my goals and attracting people and circumstances that perpetuate the cycle. I'm ready to deal with my real needs in a real way and to free myself to work toward my goal for the joy *of sharing my gifts and creating wealth."*

After doing this exercise, you're ready to use Tapping to start dismantling this hidden agenda and negative cycle. It can be used to both clear negatives and enhance and solidify "aha" moments. I highly recommend that you voice this round loudly and use your own words when you can.

TAPPING SCRIPT TO CLARIFY AND CLEAR ANY ATTACHMENTS TO EARNING MUCH MORE MONEY

Tap through the points, using the following phrases or your own:

I really need this money! *** I need it because then I'll finally have arrived *** I'll finally feel validated *** That I *am* good enough ***

(continued)

I'll finally feel seen for my brilliance! *** It will mean something really important beyond the money *** I need it so I can be a winner *** Someone who has made it.

To finally prove to everyone *** Even myself *** That I can do it *** That I am good enough *** That I matter *** When I earn that much money *** I will finally feel safe, secure, at peace *** Can finally be free to do what I like and have what I like.

I'll finally be free to be me *** To feel powerful as me *** To care less about what anyone one else thinks *** When I earn that much money *** I'll finally prove them all wrong *** Distinguished myself as special *** Done it my way *** And proved that I am different.

Good enough *** Smart enough *** Strong enough *** I'll finally be the person that deserves the reward *** I really need that money for so many reasons *** And I'm not letting this go! *** This is my attachment to money *** My secret agenda and I'm keeping it!

Take a deep breath and let that sit for a minute. Notice any clarity and perspective you feel after that round. Observing this pattern is a huge leap forward in breaking the cycle. Then you're free to work toward your new goal in a whole new way! Complete this next round of Tapping to shift into the upside.

TAPPING SCRIPT TO SHIFT INTO THE UPSIDE

Tap through the points, using the following phrases or your own:

Wow, I've attached a pretty powerful hidden agenda to my goal *** I've probably attached this same agenda *** To all sorts of goals in the past *** It's really hard to let go of this attachment *** This need to earn money to finally feel and be something *** Safe *** Free *** Validated.

That's so important to me *** These are things I've wanted *** And needed for a lifetime! *** I've been so-o-o sure this is the correct way to see my goal and more money *** But I'm open to the idea that I can start meeting these needs more directly *** Now that I am seeing them so honestly *** Seeing them so clearly *** As I do that, I release and free my actual income goal to be fun, exciting, and full of possibility.

I am open to freeing my income goal *** To represent the things it should represent *** The truth is, growing my income by this huge amount *** Means I'll be giving my gift to many more people *** Giving my gift in a much bigger way *** Love giving my gift *** I love watching people benefit from my unique talents/product/service *** I love when they're happy *** Want it and really do benefit.

There are so many more people *** Who could benefit from the unique gifts I have *** The unique way that I do it *** I am now open to earning so much money *** Through the joy of being totally me *** Giving what I love to give in a much bigger way *** For the highest good of me *** And so many more people.

An Unusual but Effective Process to Expand Your Income: A quick exercise to see the true impact of setting bigger income goals and seeing how much YOU matter

www.TappingIntoWealth.com/Video8

9

RESISTANCE TO
SETTING BIG GOALS

T he process of setting clear goals—actually writing them down and reviewing them regularly—is one of the most universally accepted keys to success. Studies show that people who write down their goals are more likely to achieve them than those who only voice them. It sounds simple, but I've found that the vast majority of people with dreams and good ideas avoid setting goals, especially for money. They say they want to earn more or grow their business or have enough to take vacations and pay bills. But that's subjective, with no figures or details. Few people actually set a specific goal for how much they want to earn. You need to! In order to create and attract what you want in your life, your first step should be to clarify what you want and then ask for it.

Why We Avoid Setting Goals

Typically, self-employed people or small-business owners work hard setting and achieving all sorts of goals in their business every day—for product quality, manufacturing efficiency, or satisfied customers. But they often don't set concrete income goals. If you don't set specific goals, start to do it so you can transition from your old paradigm to a new wealth reality. Setting an income goal is *the* most powerful step you can take. So why don't the majority of people do it?

Setting a goal that's outside your comfort zone of know-how and confidence, which money goals often are, causes resistance that shows up as some form of uncomfortable emotion, typically fear or anxiety. It can also trigger a rush of loud and persistent thoughts like, "That's impossible" or "What if I fail?" or "That would probably be too hard and I'll never see my family." Setting an income goal and reviewing it regularly can be incredibly uncomfortable because it puts a spotlight on your inner skepticism about your own abilities and worth. It also brings up a lack of faith in whether or not dreams can come true.

As I said earlier, your current income reflects exactly where you feel you should be—the level that makes you feel safe. While consciously you may believe that where you are now doesn't work for you financially, it doesn't push the uncomfortable emotional buttons that setting big goals can. When you set a goal that's substantially beyond your current income number, you can see and feel the programming and limiting beliefs that keep your number small. This is important to understand. In previous chapters I discussed how limiting beliefs keep you small and sabotage your desire for more money. But it can be hard to recognize your personal limiting beliefs. Setting a big income goal will illuminate them and they'll suddenly become loud and clear.

When you use Tapping as a tool to clear away all that resistance, your big goal switches from being stressful to being exciting and full of possibility. Most important, your goals will begin to motivate you instead of holding you back. When you stop dwelling on how scary it feels to not know how to achieve the goal, which is usually based on what you heard and believed in the past, and slowly focus on your possibilities, your self-talk changes. You'll start to ask yourself productive questions that spark your vision: "What will my world look like?" "How could I earn that much?" "How would my business look?" "How many customers or clients would I need?"

I know how the process feels because I went through it as I built my current business. After being in practice for a year, I ran my first small workshop and taught how to set outrageous goals. I set my goal for $350,000 per year, on my way to $500,000. I needed to do lots of Tapping to eliminate the fear, panic, and disbelief I felt. Each time I felt excited about the possibility, I started to ponder the questions that I had never thought of before: "What will I do in the future to earn that much?" "How large would my workshops have to be?" "How would I attract that many people?" "What else would have to be in place?"

I closed my eyes and saw Jack Canfield on stage with thousands of people listening, and it hit me. In order to create that kind of income, I'd have to speak on what's known as "the Jack Canfield level." My entire focus shifted rapidly from what I've known, or thought I knew, to the unknown. I realized that the actions I would take to lead me to earn $100,000 a year as a practitioner would never lead to $350,000. I was a bit lost about how to proceed, but found myself drawn to read certain books, watch specific videos, and study personal development speakers.

I learned of a live workshop being offered by one of the top people in my industry that cost $1,200 for three days—more than I had ever imagined spending out of my own pocket on training. It was only an hour from home. Every time e-mails about it arrived, I felt drawn to go. After weeks of fighting it, I registered for this expensive workshop, rationalizing that I'd benefit from attending and could also learn how to run a three-day seminar. Both happened, but nothing compared to the life-altering miraculous connections I made at that event with people who changed the course of my life multiple times.

Acting spontaneously led me to the first real, solid step to earning my goal income. When you move away from a logical, analytical way of thinking, letting go of what you believe is possible from past experiences, and go to a mind-set of wondering, musing, and curiosity, miracles can happen. Creative ideas and inspired thinking flow from this place. When you go from the vibe of "It's impossible," to "There are many ways to make this happen," you step into your highest potential for inspired million-dollar ideas.

SHIFTING FROM IMPOSSIBLE TO POSSIBLE

The shift from refusing to consider a goal that's well above your current level to believing you can do it is possible because there are two parts to your mind. First, there's the analytical, logical part that's focused on implementing a step-by-step, practical plan. The other side is the non-linear, imaginative, visionary part of your mind that draws on your more unconscious creativity. When this takes over, you can make quantum leaps. Once you feel open to the possibility of succeeding and are simply curious about how it can be achieved (without getting stuck on "the how's"), you open that creative part of your mind. That unlocks a treasure chest! Each day, each time you look at your goal, you'll think: "Yes, I want that!" The creative part will see it as an interesting problem to solve and be excited to try to reach the goal.

~ *When you begin to believe that anything is possible,*
  anything is possible. ~

The creative part of your mind will begin to incubate and try to stimulate growth for the ideas and visions. You'll feel nudges to act, similar to intuition or moments of inspiration. Sometimes they won't seem logical or practical. But you'll be drawn to them and they'll keep popping up until you listen. When a goal excites you and you're open to it, you'll summon more energy, courage, and desire to take action. Once you set a specific goal and focus on it with an open vibe, you'll attract what's needed to bring it to fruition. Your focus, enthusiasm, and diligent work will rise to the level needed. In this way, a goal truly acts as a catalyst.

First answer the question: "What goal do I want to go after?" Most people set a goal that's only incrementally bigger than their current income—just within their current belief system of what's possible—and don't consider the bigger vision of what they can get if they open their minds to it. It's a good first step. But when you realize the power of what a goal draws from you and how specifically it matches what you want, think very carefully about what goal to set. Do you want to use your brilliant ideas, drive, and action to meet a goal that's just one step up from where you are now? Or do you want to match a goal that's ten steps beyond your current situation—a big, fat, outrageous goal that would rock your world if you could achieve it?

When Bethany came to me, I was impressed with her incredible talents as an interior designer. But her business was run more like a hobby. She'd considered a few goals but was always limited by what she thought she could make, based on how things had gone so far. We created goals together, starting with how much money she needed to take home to pay bills, add to her savings and retirement plans, and enjoy life. This goal represented one step up for her—short-term and modest. Bethany felt that if she could pay her bills and living expenses and have an extra $500 per month for pleasure, it would be a massive change for the better.

We scaled her monthly take-home pay number to gross business sales. Once we had a business revenue number and wrote it on paper, Bethany got visibly upset. She felt physically ill looking at it and spoke rapid fire and nervously: "I don't see how that's possible or know how to get there. Would I have to charge more? I don't know if I can. That number is very big, I don't want that much pressure!" A few rounds of Tapping shifted her into a place of calm and she became open to the options available to her that could earn that much money.

From there we mapped out exactly how many new clients she'd need to add per month. We then connected that number to a specific amount of targeted networking activities she'd have to participate in to bring in that many new clients. Tears came as Bethany looked over the plan. "I can do this, I can really do this!" she exclaimed. Bethany left with renewed excitement and focus about how many new clients she'd find. At her next networking meeting, she shared her vision. Suddenly, colleagues stepped up with referrals and ideas to help meet the goal. Within six months, she added the exact number of new clients that she'd outlined in her plan.

GETTING EXCITED

I recommend that you set a short-term goal and an outrageously big one too. Here's what will happen, so you're prepared. When you set a goal that's an incremental step up from your current income or a large step up, you'll get ideas, inspirations, nudges to act that seem practical and on track to that goal. You might even call them obvious steps. When you set an outrageous goal that's far beyond your current earnings, the ideas, inspirations, and nudges to act may seem strange or counterintuitive, like my draw to the workshop many years ago. It's often hard to see how they're connected to the outrageous goal at all.

Following this kind of enlightenment takes more faith. Achieving an outrageous goal requires a huge swing in your thinking, actions, and even your self-identity. Being aware that it takes lots of faith will help keep you on track and moving forward.

There's another side to what happens when you set outrageous goals with excitement behind them. Things can get interesting in a good way. Some credit it to the Law of Attraction; others to miracles aligning. I call it "unexpected synchronicities." When you set a goal and get excited, it often seems like reality itself shifts in your favor. Unexpected connections may suddenly start to appear out of nowhere with perfect timing to support you on the journey to your goal. You'll say things like: "What a coincidence"; "I can't believe it happened"; "What are the chances of that showing up?" It can feel miraculous!

The Law of Attraction perspective is that when you become clear about your goal and have feelings of excitement and anticipation around it, you become a more powerful magnet and draw everything you need to make the goal real. There are many theories about how this works. The important thing is that it happens. You've probably experienced this if you've been excited about something you want. Being totally on fire can make it feel like the world is conspiring to support you, with perfect timing. People may say, "It's like the stars were aligned." But it's not the stars. Good things come when your beliefs, your enthusiasm, your expectations, and your level of deserving feelings are aligned after you've cleared negative emotions attached to them. Just as negative emotions block desires, replacing them with positive ones can fuel them.

Part of this process is how you use your voice. When you're excited about a goal, you start talking about it. You may not mention the amount of money you want, but you do share thoughts about growing the business side of a goal or helping more people by expanding and moving your business to the next level. When you talk about income or business growth, people hear and respond to the special tone of positive energy in your voice. The feeling behind your message is the single most important thing that can transform goals into reality. You know that special quality as enthusiasm. When you enthusiastically speak about your goal, your vision, and your contribution, people want to support and be around you. Enthusiasm is contagious and people are drawn to the vision that motivates it.

BIG GOAL ADVANTAGES

Society bombards us with so much programming against taking a new path; yet people are still naturally attracted to the possibility, vision, excitement, and curiosity of "What if?" questions. When you enthusiastically share your vision with friends, colleagues, customers, employees, and prospective clients, you'll enroll supporters, followers, and investors. This is when circumstances, resources, and ideas start to come through other people and their networks. It's amazing how supportive people become when you share the bigger vision and intentions around your goals. Sometimes it happens so fast it becomes obvious how much you were *not* doing until now.

All these great opportunities become feasible when you have a goal and allow yourself to shift from resistance to excited possibility and become vocal about it. For example, John was the new owner of a small business he'd taken over when he came to me. He quickly discovered that employee relations had been handled badly by the previous owner. He wanted a fresh start with his staff and quickly turned things around. They began to like him and feel happier with a boss who supported them. But eventually John realized they weren't motivated or interested in doing more than the basic requirements of their jobs, and there were often power struggles over who was responsible for doing what that caused delays in getting products out on time.

John worked fourteen-hour days and had to constantly micromanage. When I first encouraged him to set goals, he responded negatively. His fears and limiting beliefs made him nervous. One of his strongest blocks was believing he had to do everything important himself, which explained his long work hours. Past experiences made him hesitant to trust employees with critical tasks. Once we Tapped on these past experiences, he was more open to creating goals for his second and fifth year marks at the business. We worked together to make sure the goals felt exciting and motivated him to do what was necessary, instead of making him scared to take action.

But he didn't share this with his employees. It was his little secret, since it represented his overall business revenue and what he'd personally earn, although he felt comfortable communicating his more general, long-term goals to colleagues and investors. But without knowing his vision, his employees had no way to connect with a common mission or goal. Their individual functions felt meaningless without a full picture. They didn't feel part of something bigger. Instead it felt like they worked just to do a task that meant nothing more than a paycheck.

I worked with John to expand his income number in a way that incorporated a more holistic view of his business. By visualizing the company operating at his goal level of sales and profitability, we could project and estimate what that could mean for employees. They'd get many positive benefits if he reached his goal, including job security, overtime pay, opportunity for advancement, profit sharing, and the like. To meet his aggressive sales goals, the company would also have to emerge as a brand of quality, innovation, and craftsmanship. I asked, "What would that mean to the employees?" John realized that by sharing this vision with them, all the hard work would make sense and motivate them to want the company to do well.

John's final concern in sharing the vision was: "But I can't promise this will happen. And I'm not even sure how to get there." John was shocked when I suggested he share that too. Sharing your vision is not a promise. It's an objective that must be presented with honesty, humanity, and integrity. View your goal as an inspirational image of the future. Big—especially outrageously big—goals inspire, motivate, and unite people in a shared mission. The very fact that you don't know exactly how to get there invites innovation and focus from everyone, which happened for John. Sharing his goals and vision for the company and his intention for the employees became one of the most powerful, defining moments in his life.

John made a life-changing speech, in an open and honest way, revealing his plans for the business and how it could affect everyone working for him. The response was immediate and dramatic. The staff was captivated and wanted to know how they could help meet the goal.

They started volunteering ideas and innovations in each area of the business. Everything changed that day. Their level of motivation, teamwork, and initiative all dramatically changed. John identified and promoted several people to enhance the business and drastically reduced his own hours. This allowed him to start spending more time with his family and allowed his employees to become full participants in a team working on a shared mission.

There are many upsides to having a goal for your income, even if it feels uncomfortable at first. If thinking about great big, outrageous, scary goals triggers great big, scary emotions, you'll avoid even considering making an attempt to bring them to fruition and won't talk about them, which doesn't attract support. When you clear your limiting and negative beliefs and voice your goal out loud with vision and enthusiasm, miracles happen! Those miracles can appear from inside of you as well as through other people, circumstances, and unexpected coincidences that brilliantly align to make your goal happen quickly and directly.

The first thing you must do is use Tapping to clear away all the negative stuff that comes up so you can completely shift your vibe about your goal. Tapping allows you to look at your goal and transform it from feeling stressful and uncomfortable to feeling incredibly excited and full of possibly. When that happens, be prepared for miracles!

CLEARING RESISTANCE TO SETTING BIG GOALS

One of the first things that comes up when you set a big money goal is a feeling of disbelief that this is even remotely possible. To get started, write down the amount of money you'd ideally love to have as your goal and say out loud, "I can't achieve this goal. It's impossible!" Tune in to that number as you say it and measure on a scale of 1 to 10 how true that feels right now, not how you want it to feel. Start Tapping on your belief about whether you think your goal is even remotely possible.

TAPPING SCRIPT FOR OUTRAGEOUS
GOAL EMOTIONS #1

Tap through all the points, using the following phrases:

It's impossible *** No way! *** No how! *** It's crazy! It's too much!
*** This goal is too big! *** I can never earn that much *** Who
would ever pay me that much?

It's impossible *** I know it's impossible *** I believe that this is
impossible *** It's way too big *** It's too big for the Law of Attraction *** No one has ever made this much money *** Well, some
people have.

But not me! *** Not in a million years *** It's impossible *** I
can predict the future with accuracy *** And I know what's going to
happen *** And I'm telling you there's no way this is possible ***
There's no way this will ever come to pass.

Take a nice deep breath and rate the belief again—"I can't achieve
this goal. It's impossible!" Measure on a scale of 1 to 10 how true that
feels after doing that Tapping round. Write down any thoughts or
memories that come up and change the script to include them in your
Tapping. Do this round again and again, voicing all your logical resistance until the statement "It's impossible!" feels less true and your goal
feels a little more believable. Ideally it should feel true between no more
than zero and three. When you're feeling more neutral about these
emotions, do the second round in a positive frame.

TAPPING SCRIPT FOR OUTRAGEOUS GOAL EMOTIONS #2

Tap through all the points, using the following phrases:

I still don't believe it's completely possible *** I mean, it seems crazy *** But I'm choosing to be open *** To the limitless possibilities of the universe *** Beyond what I can currently see *** I am somehow having faith *** That everything I need to accomplish this goal *** Will surprise me by occurring in the right way at the right time.

Isn't it wonderful when resources appear? *** Impossible things happen every day *** What if I could just open myself up to the possibility *** And focus on it with a positive intent *** Allowing it to come into my reality *** As crazy as that sounds? *** Maybe I choose to be crazy! *** I choose to be crazy!

Take a nice deep breath. How do you feel about setting a great big outrageous goal now? Notice how much more excitement you are feeling about what's possible!

HOW MUCH MONEY IS ENOUGH?

It's important to put thought into deciding *very specifically* how much income you want. Some people pick a huge number out of the air, like a million dollars. If yours is so far out of the realm of your present reality or talents, it won't create any beliefs or resistance. Instead, it becomes "if I could only win the lottery" wishful thinking that you don't give much credence to. And if your number just helps you break even, or get a tiny step above that, you fall into the "I just need enough to get by" mentality. It's important to choose your income goal carefully.

You should also be careful about not buying into any belief that asking for more than you need is selfish. That mentality keeps you from asking for lots of money, and the Law of Attraction supports your belief to get just enough. For example, when Gina came to my workshop, I asked where she thought her blocks came from. She insisted she had none. She grew up with loving parents who had a decent income, but then mentioned that her mom tried not to spend much. After going from very well off to poor when her father lost his business, Gina's mom grew up believing you can never have enough money saved.

Gina proudly stated she was the opposite of her frugal, fearful mom. She was very spiritual, never worried about money, and always had enough, despite being a freelance photographer with no guaranteed income. I pointed out that she was so focused on always having enough that the universe heard she didn't need more. Yet she got emotional about setting a higher goal, as though it were greedy. Her "aha" moment was recognizing her biggest block—focusing on needing just enough to pay bills and have some for fun. Once she cleared that belief with Tapping, her income goals got much higher, as did her income.

Big income goals crystallize your resistance. Nothing pushes more buttons, challenges your beliefs, or feels more uncomfortable than setting a big income goal. It's time to stop thinking small and settling for incremental increases in your income! To greatly increase it, you need to create an income goal that far exceeds what you earn now. Consider an income number that's impossible to reach if you just continue working harder, with longer hours and incremental improvements.

Are you wondering, "Is it okay to be so focused on money?" The actual process of setting a big income goal can sound materialistic, unenlightened, selfish, or even wrong. Pay close attention to any button that's pushed and deal with it quickly. If a bigger money goal is fueled by a desire for something you want to buy—things you can't afford now—or a desire to gain less tangible benefits like freedom, security, joy, and the ability to relax, that might seem selfish. It may feel better if your big income goal is tied to something more altruistic, like wanting to support a charitable cause. That may align more with your heart, purpose, and maybe religion. It will serve you well if you allow it to overlay your income goals. But don't just think in terms of either/or—having lots of money to spend on your pleasure *or* lots to give for charity. You count just as much as others and can increase your income enough to buy what you'd like and help others too!

~ Money allows you to live at the fullest expression of your creativity, productivity, and generosity. ~

Think about how much more good you could do for the world if you had twice as much income. Would you be empowered to do more for yourself and also donate more? What would three times as much income allow you to have? Would you love the freedom of having more time to get involved with causes that matter to you? If so, then how can you serve these causes if you consider having lots of money to be selfish, materialistic, or sinful? Isn't it more selfish to keep yourself small when many people could benefit from your talents? Without money, you can't live at the fullest expression of your creativity, productivity, and joy. Without money, you can't live at the fullest expression of your compassion, generosity, or life's purpose. You deserve to be able to have enough for it all!

Supercharge Your Income Goals by Aligning With Miracles: A must-see Tapping exercise that will bring you into the "miracle vibe" www.TappingIntoWealth.com/Video9

10

SETTING
OUTRAGEOUS
GOALS

W hy don't I have more money?" After reading the previous chapters, you should have a good idea about what's been blocking your ability to improve your financial picture. Now it's time to start setting outrageously big goals! They'll make you question your belief in yourself, your ability to accomplish what you want, and your faith in such idealistic notions as "Dreams can come true." Yet these buttons need to be pushed to find all your subconscious reasons for not making more money. Setting goals that push those buttons allow you to break through the resistance that keeps you stuck in a place with less money than you'd like. We're going to do a lot of Tapping in this chapter, as it's critical to get past the blocks that keep you from setting the outrageous goals necessary for making a lot more money.

Creating an Outrageous Income Goal

I want to take you through a more disciplined process to help you clarify what you want more money for and ensure that you're reaching for a goal that goes beyond debt repayment or breaking even. Creating a solvency income goal is necessary to achieve this. This is a figure that allows you to save, invest, *and* enjoy life. When you create an income goal, it should always include the amount of money needed for the things you want in life—to live the way you choose, not settle for.

List all of your monthly expenses, including current fixed payments like a mortgage or rent, insurance, car payments, utilities, etc. Also include your desired expenses for things like college funds, retirement, or debt repayment. Don't forget to include a savings account contribution. This list should contain everything related to your and your family's financial well-being and future. Next comes the part that may kick up some uncomfortable emotions. Add to that the monthly amount of money needed to do *all* the things that would make your life enjoyable. Be generous with yourself! The end result of this process is an income goal number.

Now take a long, hard look at that goal number and remind yourself of how you came up with it. Write that number big and bold across a page. Pay attention to how uncomfortable you get and how much resistance you start to feel as you focus on it. Notice any emotions and feelings in your body that come up, such as your stomach going into knots. Think about how it would feel to announce your new income goal to your friends and family. Any resistance you feel reflects your fears, limiting beliefs, and intentions that counter what you say you want. It's your subconscious saying, "*No*, this is not viable!" to achieving the income goal.

Now take a deep breath and double this goal number. Are you screaming "This is impossible!" yet? Look at the doubled goal and notice how your emotions can intensify. Are you thinking "This is ridiculous!" or maybe, "It would take a miracle!" When those thoughts and feelings get strong, you've found your outrageous goal. In order to actually reach it, a miraculous amount of brilliance has to come from within you. You'll need inspired ideas and creativity. You'll also have to raise your level of action, leadership, confidence, and execution to meet this goal. Reaching it requires finding people, resources, information, ideas, circumstances, and opportunities to line up with the perfect timing to support you. Just imagine that unfolding! Are you still saying "Impossible"? It's not.

Since an outrageous goal can seem too much, it's important to have short-term goals as steps to reach it. Remind yourself often that the journey to your outrageous goal is one worth taking, since it's also the journey to *you*: your life, passion, and purpose are calling you to grow, expand, and become more than you've ever been. Wouldn't it feel wonderful to experience having all the money and success you dreamed of and be the bold, brilliant, and amazing person who created it? That's why I told you to double your goal. You must think big if you want a lot more money. *Outrageous success starts with an outrageous goal!*

Let's do some Tapping on how you feel about that income number and the emotions that came up. Since it's way more than you've ever made, it can be hard to believe it's possible to make that kind of money, which makes resistance to it slightly different from other kinds of blocks. Look at that number and pay attention to how you feel about this sentence: *It's way more than I've ever made.* Rate your discomfort and how strongly you feel about not being able to reach that level of income on a scale from 1 to 10 before you do the next round of Tapping.

TAPPING SCRIPT FOR OUTRAGEOUS GOAL EMOTIONS

Say the following phrases aloud while tapping on the karate chop point:

Even though I'm not sure about this, I don't know what it would be like, or how hard it will be to get there, I choose to have faith that I'm following my intention. And my intention is to step each day into my life's purpose with passion and with joy. My intention is to become more *me* than I have ever been, surrounded by the people and the things that bring me joy. Maybe that's what it will be like. As I let go of any beliefs or programming that says I need to struggle, I align with my passion and my joy.

Tap through all the points, using the following phrases:

It's too much *** It can't happen *** What could I possibly do to earn that? *** I don't know what that would be like *** It's way more than I have ever earned! *** Maybe it would be really hard *** It's just too big *** It's a number that's almost unachievable.

I can't imagine it *** What could I do that could have that much value? *** Why do I even need that much money? *** It's just too much *** It seems like it might be really hard *** It will probably require a ton of work *** It's just too much and it would be just too hard.

Take a nice, deep breath and measure your discomfort level again. Don't move on until you're at 3 or less. Write down any thoughts, feelings, or memories that come up. There may be physical sensations as well. Each of these can be addressed in your own words with separate Tapping sessions.

Once you've calmed your negative emotions, move to this positive round.

POSITIVE TAPPING FOR OUTRAGEOUS GOALS

Continue Tapping through all the points, using the following phrases:

I'm not sure about this *** I still think it might be really hard to get there *** I choose to have faith *** That I am following my intention *** And my intention is *** To step each day into my life's purpose *** Yes, into my life's purpose with passion *** And with joy *** My intention is to become more of *me* *** Than I have ever been *** My intention is to be surrounded *** By the people and things that bring me joy.

As I let go of any beliefs or programming *** That say I need to struggle *** Or that belief that it's necessary to struggle *** I align with my passion *** I align with my joy *** I choose to align with my intention *** I choose to allow my subconscious mind *** To make the connection between what my goal is *** And me surrounded by people and things that bring me joy *** I love allowing into my life *** More people and more things *** That bring me joy *** I am choosing to have faith *** That I am following my positive intention.

Take a deep breath. You might want to do this more times until you feel more centered and have a sense of peace about your goal.

NURTURING YOUR INNER ENTREPRENEUR

If you're self-employed or own a small business, it's imperative to set your personal income goal first. Decide how much money your business has to pour into your life for you to be happy and have financial freedom. Use this number to set your business goals, not the other way around. Many people set personal income goals based on beliefs about what their business has achieved so far and how much more they think it can take in. This thinking will limit both you and your business.

Your personal income and time/freedom goals for three, five, and ten years from now should create the revenue goals for your business three, five, and ten years from now so everything you do can line up with that goal. Your brilliance and the Law of Attraction will support this. But many business owners never take this critical goal-setting step because of limiting beliefs and resistance. When you have no goal for both your personal and your business needs, all your actions, inspirations, and tactics default to the model of the past, which keeps you stuck. That means in three, five, and ten years, you'll have the same income, work hours, and lack of freedom as you do today.

I've coached many business owners who lived this story and are physically, emotionally, and even spiritually exhausted. What began as their life's dream that would allow them freedom turned into 24/7 enslavement. So unless that's what you want, get these goals down! Think big, write them down, and know that Tapping helps you to move through each goal. Don't forget, you now have a secret weapon at your fingertips! Outrageous goals trigger the visionary mind of the entrepreneur to great progress. Nourish and encourage the entrepreneur in you or you'll revert back to, "I don't know how to get there," and stop thinking big.

Your analytical mind isn't comfortable with a stretch goal—one you can't just get to by incrementally working more—because it wants to know all the steps to get there, and likely doesn't know how to reach an outrageous one. That's natural, since the mind only knows the past. If you keep doing the same thing, you get the same thing. So not knowing how to reach a goal this big is why you need it. Understanding that you can't get there by just working more ensures that you'll *have* to grow, stretch, change, and leave your comfort zone for the *huge* payoff in the outrageous zone! I recommend that you start on the ten-year goal and envision, dream, and wonder. If you have a business, think about:

- What will my business do to earn that much in ten years?
- What will it look like? How will it be run?
- How many people will work for me?
- Why will customers love to buy from me?

If you have a salaried job or some other way you earn your income, consider:

- What position will I hold?
- What company will I be working for?
- Will I change course and do something that uses my skills and talents more?
- What will make me so valuable that I am paid on that level?

Then let the ten-year goal create the five-year goal and ask the same questions: "What will my business have to be in five years to get that big in ten?" Then let the five-year goal set the three-year goal. Suddenly everything you do tomorrow will be aligning with the three-, five-, and ten-year goals. At this point, there's something exciting for your brilliance to work on!

Be proactive about consciously nourishing the entrepreneur in you. Spend time each week purposely sitting in the entrepreneurial mind-set picturing and dreaming. Whether you take an hour or even ten minutes, that's more visionary thinking than 90 percent of small-business owners and solo-preneurs (individuals in business on their own) do in six months. And if you're really committed to succeed as a business owner, two of the best investments you can make are reading *The E-Myth* by Michael Gerber and hiring a business coach who knows your niche.

INCOME GOAL EXERCISES

These exercises will help you to think about the goal you want and identify your resistance to it. Create a true solvency income goal. Take every expense into account, both practical and for pleasure. Remember to make it a stretch goal. It should be somewhat believable, but at the same time, really push your buttons because it'll be challenging to actually achieve it.

Exercise for Income Goal #1: Set Your Goal

Write down "I want my income to be $_____ in ___ years." Go big! Read it out loud and pay attention to how uncomfortable just stating this goal makes you feel. This is your immediate resistance. Rate how uncomfortable you feel about it on a scale of 1 to 10, and next to your income goal, write, "My resistance to this is_____."

Think about your goal and how it makes you feel. Give yourself time to absorb it. Then move to Income Goal Exercise 2.

Exercise for Income Goal #2: State Your Disbelief

Write down three reasons why this goal is crazy and unrealistic; why it can't happen. Be as negative as you can about the reasons you have trouble believing your goal is possible. For example:

- *In my field, there's a lot of competition with fewer customers.*
- *I already work very long hours, so I don't know what else to do.*
- *It's a terrible economy so it's stupid to expect to make money.*
- *If I raise my prices to make more money, I'd lose the customers I have.*
- *My company has frozen salaries and I'm stuck with mine.*

Write down all your reasons, however many you have. You can do this over a few days to give yourself more time to think about it.

If you don't have many reasons, dig a bit. Be honest with yourself. You might be surprised to recognize what your subconscious whispers when you pay attention. This list is only for you, so nothing is too silly or embarrassing. When you've identified as many reasons as you can, move on to Income Goal Exercise 3.

Exercise for Income Goal #3: List Your Obstacles

Identify the two biggest obstacles that block your desired income goal. One should be a concrete, real-world obstacle or person. The other should be something inside of you, like a behavior or an attribute. Choose what triggers an immediate reaction of anger, annoyance, or frustration.

Obstacle Outside You: Think of something or someone (or more than one) that you can't stand and that trips you up and undermines you and your efforts. What seems to get in your way or sets you off just thinking about it? For example:

- *I can't do anything until the right circumstances happen.*
- *_____ is always critical and weakens my attempts to succeed.*
- *Paperwork wastes all my time.*

Write down your outside obstacle(s): "My obstacle(s) outside me is/are _____."

Obstacle Inside You: Think of one or more things about yourself that drive you crazy or frustrate you. It could be a step you don't or won't do, or you believe you don't do well. Maybe it embarrasses you. For example:

- *I've never been good at _____.*
- *I tend to screw up when I try to_____ so why bother trying?*
- *My nerves get the best of me when I make a big effort and that makes a bad impression.*

Write down your inside obstacle(s): "My obstacle(s) inside me is/are _____."

The next round of Tapping is for obstacles in your way. Think about the immediate ones that came up in the exercises you just did. Really focus on them. Rate on a scale of 1 to 10 how big they seem in your mind or your emotional response when thinking: *I have all these obstacles in the way of my income goals!*

TAPPING SCRIPT FOR INCOME
GOAL OBSTACLES

Tap through all the points, using the following phrases:

These obstacles *** They feel insurmountable *** Because they are insurmountable *** Boy, are they blocking me *** Boy, is it frustrating *** Boy, do they make me feel stuck *** They're blocking my progress *** If only they would just disappear out of my way.

It's all because of these obstacles *** As a matter of fact, I would be so much further ahead if it weren't for them *** These obstacles, they're huge! *** They're so frustrating *** I feel helpless when I think about these obstacles *** They're really making me stuck *** It's a no-win situation *** And I don't know how to solve this.

Take a nice deep breath. Rate how you feel now when you think about the obstacles you identified. Repeat that process until the importance or size of these obstacles start to come down and seem less important. Bring it down to 3 or less. You might have to focus on one obstacle at a time. Address whatever comes to mind. Be gentle with yourself. Take the opportunity here to list your obstacles and the feelings they trigger so you have a foundation for more clearing. When you feel ready, do this positive round.

Tap through all the points, using the following phrases:

I've got these obstacles *** I guess everyone has them *** I still can't really solve them in this moment *** I release my need to push against them *** And my need to hold on to them *** I'm choosing to dissolve these conflicts *** For my own highest good *** For the highest good of everyone involved.

I now look for unexpected avenues suddenly opening up *** I

look for doors suddenly opening to even better results *** As a matter of fact *** I am watching in amazement *** As these conflicts, somehow, easily and quietly just fade away *** They just seem less important *** I'm not going to let these old things stop me *** I am on my way *** These old conflicts are getting quieter and dimmer and just fading away.

Take a nice deep breath. Make a note of how you feel now about the challenges you face compared to when you started this process. It's important (and fun) to see your progress as you Tap through your blocks and then move forward with a bigger and better perspective.

DISPLAY YOUR NUMBER

Now that you have an outrageous income number and are uncomfortable with the idea of going after it, let's magnify the experience. Write that number down on many sticky notes, in multiple ways—the annual and monthly gross, the approximate monthly net and difference from your current monthly net. Really think about the positive benefits of having a larger net income for your life in general, including less stress about money and the means to do activities you love. Picture the money in your bank account. How quickly can you pay off debt? How will it feel to see it come in? What will the pile of money look like after six months at that income? What could you spend it on?

Place the sticky notes all over your home. This will garner an incredibly powerful resource in a completely effortless way—using your subconscious mind. At first, when you see those notes, they'll push buttons and create discomfort, which is good. You'll notice all sorts of objections in your thoughts that sound logical, but are based on emotion and shine a light on your resistance. Eventually, you'll notice them less as they shift to the periphery of your thoughts. When you stop noticing them, it means your mind has accepted them as part of your current reality. This engages the subconscious mind like a puzzle to be solved. The most brilliant, creative, and action-generating part of your mind will work on your behalf, trying to create that reality, even while you are sleeping. Don't deprive yourself of this free, effortless, and powerful resource!

Pay close attention to anything that feels like resistance. It may manifest as anticipatory embarrassment as you put up notes with your goals clearly on them. Your embarrassment will increase when people notice them and ask, "What's this?" Are they shocked, embarrassed for you, annoyed, scoffing, or condemning? This is a very interesting experiment. It will provide you with lots of information about both your resistance to making more money and how other people contribute to it.

I know how helpful this can be because I resisted setting an outrageous income goal for my own business for a long time. When I finally did, I had to practically force myself to write the numbers down and fight the urge to lower them to more comfortable levels. Embarrassment kicked in. I worried about what my family, who came over often, would think, so I put up just one note on my mirror. When my ten-year-old daughter asked what it meant, I stammered, then felt silly, realizing she was too young to understand income numbers and had no judgments or negative associations. She accepted my explanation as "Mommy's goal for earning money."

Then she surprised me by making more notes, placing them all through the house so I could see them more often. Now I was stuck since I couldn't hurt her feelings and didn't want to negatively program her attitude toward money! I had to live with my secret outrageous income numbers plastered for everyone to see, question, and judge. Resistant emotions bombarded me whenever I saw them: embarrassment, disbelief, even a sense of failure. The discouraging weight of not believing I could reach goals that were in my face constantly consumed me. I had my own judgments and expected others to think I was selfish, money-grubbing, conceited, and arrogant, and that they would ask who I thought I was to expect so much money.

Those little sticky notes pushed many buttons I'd never experienced. Thankfully I was already an EFT practitioner and recognized that each was a Tappable issue. With the help of Tapping, I got used to the uncomfortable feelings and began explaining to people that I was practicing what I preached in goal setting, and those many sticky notes were intended mainly for my subconscious mind. The embarrassment left and was replaced by feelings of inspiration and empowerment every time I saw or explained them.

Ideas began to come quickly and I completely changed my thoughts and priorities. I was drawn to resources that made crystal-clear sense in furthering my goals. Great ideas flowed and compelled me to act on them. I worked harder than ever, pushing my limits and challenging myself. But it wasn't a struggle and felt good, since I was excited to see the results. Tapping helped me conquer each challenge and clear any resistance or feelings of being overwhelmed. Slowly the universe started lining up for me. Unexpected events offered opportunities and validation that aligned with my goals.

I was on fire and had to learn how to be in high-octane mode without carrying all that excited tension and adrenaline in my body. Tapping helped with that. People and resources appeared and graciously and generously supported everything I did. It was miraculous! I came up with my approaches to this work to support my own process and my clients. My life completely changed in a year. And yes, I believe it all got started with those sticky notes and a little help from my precious daughter.

START TO TAKE CONTROL

Once you've set a big goal, the next step is to confront immediate external obstacles, like dealing with a person who sabotages you or having debt. Those are usually things you consciously live with that keep you powerfully and emotionally focused on the present reality. That's not good! You want to leave this reality since it's the result of thoughts and actions that come from your past. Present reality can only change when you do. Remember, you create your future with your present moments. Unless you want to continue living like you have in the past, stop going there!

I admit that it's easy to say but can be hard to do. Yet you must get beyond the in-your-face reality of immediate frustrations to begin this work. Even if nothing changes instantaneously, when you reduce the emotional intensity and importance of your current reality, you become freer to deal with it more calmly and to focus on your goals with more energy and positive beliefs. Begin to address your immediate beliefs so you can feel better about your outrageously big goal. If you don't take at least some control, you'll find yourself backing your goal down to smaller and smaller numbers.

To summarize, in order to set a big goal and make it happen, it's important to change the dynamics of your immediate circumstances and beliefs, such as:

- **Your immediate belief that nothing in your goal is remotely possible.** Your analytical mind can take a long time to see how a goal can take flight, or you may get overwhelmed thinking about it and give up before beginning.
- **Your immediate identification of someone or something you believe is in your way.** This brings up negative emotions, especially anger, frustration, or resentment.
- **Your immediate feelings and thoughts about a perceived shortcoming you have sabotage or block you.** You see faults or things missing in you that stand in the way of getting the success you want, and it brings up painful emotions related to feeling inadequate.
- **Your current lack of time or energy makes it difficult to imagine doing more.** It can seem too exhausting to even think

about putting in the work you imagine it would take to reach your goal.

- **Your financial debt situation**. This can overwhelm your progress with strong negative emotions and make feeling very solvent hopeless.

It's critical to address the immediate disbelief and emotional resistance to your goal with Tapping or you'll get stuck there. So do it! Stop gazing longingly and dreaming about what could be, and face the beliefs that have blocked you from making more money. You'll be amazed at how irrational and senseless they are when you look at them through the lens of Tapping. Once you do, you'll be truly free to choose your own truths and path.

"BUT—I DON'T KNOW HOW TO GET THERE . . ."

Sometimes a very big goal causes conflicts if you don't know what you have to do to reach it. Your analytical mind can get in your way if a big goal requires lots of out-of-the-box ideas, creativity, inspiration, and synchronicities. When you put this outrageous goal down on paper, there's no way you'll figure out how to get there in that minute—or even in the next days, weeks, or months—which can make it feel more impossible. This next round of Tapping is important for moving past these doubts and getting relief from your analytical mind. First, address these statements:

- "I don't know how to get there."
- "I have to figure it all out."

Say them out loud and with feeling and rate how uncomfortable they make you on a scale of 1 to 10. Then do this round of Tapping about how to figure out how to reach your goal.

TAPPING SCRIPT FOR FIGURING OUT
HOW TO REACH YOUR GOALS

Tap through all the points, using the following phrases:

I would love to focus on this goal *** But I don't know how to make it happen! *** I need to see how to do this! *** I can't figure it out! *** I don't know how all this would work *** It feels like I need to figure it all out right now *** Because if I can't figure it out, I shouldn't write down this goal *** Don't know how to make that number happen *** It's really big and I don't know how to get there *** My thoughts are racing about how I'm going to get there.

I've got to figure it out *** Maybe I should start making hundreds of "To Do" lists *** I've got to figure this out now *** Otherwise it doesn't make sense to have a goal this big *** I'm just setting myself up for failure *** If I'm putting down a goal I don't know how to achieve *** And I don't know how to achieve this goal! *** I need to figure it all out!

Take a deep breath. Pay attention to whether the intensity of your knee-jerk reaction is dropping off. Write down any pesky thoughts, feelings, sensations, and memories that still come up. Be gentle with yourself. Don't move forward until you can repeat, "I don't know how to get there. I have to figure it all out," and the truth meter is below a 3. Once you're there, do a round that's reframed with a super positive take, designed to make you feel awesome.

Tap through all the points, using the following phrases:

But I don't know how to get there! *** *It's not my job to figure out the how's* *** *Yes, it is!!* *** No, it isn't!! *** I have faith that the universe *** Will rearrange itself to make it happen for me *** In the shortest, quickest, most harmonious way for me *** Somehow I will attract the way.

And the way will show up *** I will be surprised and dazzled by what is delivered to me *** What if all my actions are inspired actions *** And I know when and how to take them? *** What if all I need to do is have faith each day? *** All I need to do is focus on my goal *** And have faith that the universe will line itself up for me *** Wouldn't that be wonderful?

Of course it will be wonderful *** I'm allowing my faith to send a message to the universe *** I'm ready for your help *** I'm ready for you to line up the how's! *** As you line up the how's for me *** I will take inspired action *** I do love having brilliant ideas *** I do love taking inspired action *** I'm allowing the universe to rearrange itself for me *** And I'm surprised and delighted by what it brings.

Take a nice deep breath. Do this round a few times until you feel good about your goal. Most people report feeling charged up after this round of Tapping. Once you've done it enough to feel like you're in a good place to set your goals, read on to learn how to find your way to making the goal a reality!

Developing the Midas Touch in Everything You Do: A new understanding of the power of inspired action and fast Tapping to keep you moving forward www.TappingIntoWealth.com/Video10

11

GOAL TRAUMA

J ust as having a past event related to your finances is called "financial trauma," you can have a "goal trauma" that casts a dark cloud over every aspect of your new goal and your willingness to really go after it! What defines a past experience as a goal trauma? I view it as any experience from the past that leaves you with:

- An increased level of distress, anxiety, and/or regret when you recall it
- Increased stress and a tendency to overreact when a current situation feels similar
- A great loss of your personal power in the form of trust, confidence, and belief

Identifying Goal Traumas

A goal trauma typically occurs after you want something very badly but it falls apart after you did everything you could to make it happen.

The demise of this goal might have come in a very unexpected way, so you weren't prepared for failure. Goal trauma tends to occur when you set your heart on something and you let yourself follow your dream, think big, and believe it will happen, ignoring naysayers and your own internal skeptic. You work extremely hard to achieve it, even to the point of exhaustion.

Sacrifices made along the way come at a steep personal price. You might have lost money you couldn't afford to lose, damaged relationships because of your focus on your goal, and compromised your health as a result of stress, exhaustion, and neglecting your well-being. You convince yourself that it will be worth it in the end. But despite hard work and sacrifice, things go terribly wrong. Not only does your dream not come true, but you also experience painful loss and feel like a failure. It ends with disappointment, disillusionment, self-criticism, and sadness. After an event like that, you tend to:

- Trust yourself less
- Trust other people and the universe less
- Be more skeptical of the idea that anything is possible

If you can think of a past situation that sounds like a version of what I just described, you have a goal trauma. That can make you much more conservative about thinking big and cause you to avoid getting your hopes up when setting goals. When you have goal trauma, it looms darkly as a cautionary tale of what can go wrong and the mistakes you might make as you set a new income goal. Instead of approaching it with a fresh and willing attitude, you'll have a higher level of stress and anxiety, be less resilient when challenges occur, and feel a personal power shortage.

Goal trauma causes you to approach new goals with hesitation and doubt. Rather than jump into action, you'll procrastinate, take half-hearted steps to your new goal, or be indecisive about what to do. Even if you're willing to set a goal, a power shortage will prevent you from wanting it enough to go after it with all you have. Why pursue a goal if you don't trust yourself or you believe it's impossible based on your experience in the past? You might even be conscious of holding yourself back, but think you're being practical by doing so. Take the example of Arthur, who came to me because his business was stuck and he had barely made ends meet for several years.

As we worked on creating big new goals and visions for his business, his energy was totally lackluster. No matter what I tried during the goal setting we did, I couldn't get even a small spark of excitement from him. He acquiesced to my suggestions by nodding and shrugging his shoulders. When I asked him about it, he said, "Well, I am not going to get all gung ho about it now. Let's just see what happens." When I explained that bold changes and dramatically increased income wouldn't happen with a "Let's see what happens" attitude, his lack of interest increased. So I asked what he saw as the downside of getting gung ho about a new goal for his business.

Arthur admitted that years before, when he was still an athletic coach, he had a genius idea for a product that could transform the mechanics of athletes in several sports. He believed in it so much that he had a prototype made, and it worked. He then started to dream big, knowing this could revolutionize many sports. Though none of his friends or colleagues saw the potential, he decided to go for it and spent the next three years working long days at his job, then working late into the night on his invention. He invested his own money and convinced friends and local businesses to invest too, found a partner to help sell the product, and used weekend and vacation time to try to sell it. Arthur would sometimes barely sleep for weeks, but his belief and excitement drove him onward.

During those three years, he missed precious time with his sons, often telling them, "Daddy has to work" when they wanted to play soccer with him after dinner. Yet, each time, he justified his actions by saying, "This will all pay off, if I can just get a bit further!" He was sure a breakthrough was right around the corner. But it never came. The prototypes were too expensive to get into the field, and the majority of coaches just could not grasp the power of the invention. Eventually, Arthur's money and energy ran out and he was forced to declare defeat. His money, and all his investors' money, was gone. His invention got put in storage. Unfortunately, the damage to his relationships was too much. He had a very heartbreaking divorce, and children whom he barely knew. And he was more trapped than ever in a job he had grown to dislike.

Arthur made a silent vow to never believe in his ideas, instincts, and dreams again. Even when he became self-employed, he vowed to stick to working hard and do everything himself so he didn't lose more money on pipe dreams. He created a business that required him to work ten hours a day, seven days a week. As we cleared his past trauma with Tapping, Arthur became overcome with grief and guilt about everything he had lost by believing in and following his dream, and recognized how he refused to ever believe in or get excited about one again. Afterward he was drained, but had a new perspective about the past ten years. He'd punished himself enough and was ready to create again, this time with the wisdom and balance of the man he was today. He left my office saying, "I haven't felt this alive in years" and was totally gung ho about the outrageous goal that represented his new dream!

CLEARING GOAL TRAUMA

If you want to succeed in your current goals, it's critical to work on any goal trauma you might have. While you can't undo the past, you can make a massive shift in how you see past events. The reality is that you learned a lot of lessons about what you're doing and about your per-ceived strengths and weaknesses through past events. Looking back, what you learned makes you better, smarter, and actually *more* likely to succeed, instead of becoming a road block for any of your efforts to suc-ceed again.

You can also recognize patterns, like self-criticism, that you slip into because of these past traumas. Putting yourself and your abilities down will almost always sabotage your success. These are incredibly impor-tant lessons! After doing the Tapping below, it's my intention that you'll be able to look back at this old event, see it through new eyes, and say, "Because of that event, I now trust myself *more*, trust the universe more, and believe this can happen!"

Exercise for Goal Trauma

Start by choosing a goal trauma story from your past. Close your eyes and imagine that event playing out in your mind, like you're watching it on TV. If this story were a mini-movie, what would its title be? The title alone often reveals how powerfully this story affects you and how much you lost. Commonly I've heard titles like, "The Day I Lost Everything," "Utter Failure," or "The Year from Hell."

How do you know if this old event causes you a power shortage for achieving your goals today? Notice how you feel about the big goal you set for yourself in chapter 10 while you think about this old event. How do the following statements feel on a scale of 1 to 10? "I really want *it!" and "I know I can do it!"*

If you don't have much feeling, excitement, or energy in either of those statements, you have your answer.

TAPPING SCRIPT FOR GOAL TRAUMA, ROUND 1

Say the following phrases aloud while tapping on the karate chop point:

Even though I have this story and it's a horror show, I love and accept myself with compassion, because carrying this is heavy.

Even though I have this story and it's full of pain and judgment and sadness, I totally honor myself. Honor the weight I've been carrying in this story. No one's honored me for this, not even me. I'm open to loving and accepting myself with forgiveness and compassion.

Continue Tapping through all the points, using the following phrases:

Actually, I can't forgive myself *** Because this is really bad *** And I really screwed up *** I failed *** Big time *** It's unforgivable *** It was a nightmare *** And it was so much worse.

Because I really did care *** I really did want it *** I tried to be open to miracles *** Tried to be at my best *** I tried so hard *** And I was destroyed *** So much hurt *** No one to blame but me.

I lost so much *** And it still hurts *** Utter failure *** Pain *** Sadness *** Disappointment *** I see the story *** It's a really bad movie.

But I watch it *** When I think about my goals *** Sometimes I watch this movie *** It really kicks my butt *** But right now *** I'm just going to honor this *** Honor the whole story.

Take a nice deep breath. Often, after Tapping through that round, people recognize a story like this as a type of trauma. You may see a huge charge of self-criticism appear, so I'm including a bonus round of Tapping for this event before we move on. To set you up, once again picture yourself in the movie of your past event. See yourself in the part of the story where everything is going wrong and notice if some harsh judgment is coming up in your thoughts. If so, this very harsh round of Tapping is for you. Countless numbers of people have told me these words are perfect for their inner critic concerning goal trauma. As always, replace my words with your own when you can.

TAPPING SCRIPT FOR GOAL TRAUMA, BONUS ROUND

Start Tapping through all the points, using the following phrases:

There I am *** I should have known better *** Idiot! *** Weak! *** Stupid! *** Clueless! *** I should have known better *** So trusting.

Too giving *** I really should have known better! *** So naive *** I should have figured it out *** I should have seen the signs *** I should have been stronger *** God, I'm angry at myself *** I was too trusting.

I didn't see the writing on the wall *** I just kept going *** And I deserve this judgment *** Because I'm seeing the truth *** I was an idiot *** Weak and naive! *** Should have done it better *** Should have been stronger and smarter.

I totally judge this old version of me *** And I should *** Because I'm right *** I've got a lot of evidence *** I should have done it better *** If anyone argues with me about this *** I will know they are wrong *** I was stupid, naive, and too trusting.

Take a nice deep breath. Next close your eyes and see yourself in the movie again, you will probably feel a *lot* more compassion for yourself. You may also suddenly feel extremely sad about what happened to you and how much you lost. This is where it often hits home just how much you did lose, not only in terms of external things, but also in your self-confidence and trust. So this next round is in honor of the intense emotion that can come up. Honor yourself and what you endured in the goal trauma.

TAPPING SCRIPT FOR GOAL TRAUMA, ROUND 2

Say the following phrases aloud while tapping on the karate chop point:

Even though I have this story and I've been ruthless about it, I'm just going to honor myself now. There was a lot going on. I had to handle a lot and I took it all on without a lot of support. I was doing the best I knew how.

Even though part of me, my internal critic, says, "No, I wasn't," I totally honor this old story. I was feeling a lot of pain, a lot of fear, maybe even terror. My programs and paradigms were running unconsciously. Given all that, I actually survived it pretty well. I honor myself now. I'm open to the idea that I could be proud of how I handled it.

Even though I have this old story and I would shout from the rooftops that there's not an ounce of divinity in it, I'm open to seeing the gift because I learned some important things.

Continue tapping through all the points, using the following phrases:

All this sadness *** I honor who I am *** I honor who I was in this story *** Nobody else did *** So I do now *** I had so much going

(continued)

on *** I was really doing the best I knew how *** Do I really need this judgment on top of that?

And I learned things in that event *** It made me smarter *** You bet it did! *** It made me stronger *** It gave me strength *** Because I survived it *** I came through *** I actually didn't crumble forever *** And I honor that *** I deserve that *** I'm open to seeing *** The hero in this story *** The hero was me.

Take a nice deep breath. I often ask people, "If the movie of your story were to be shown in a theater, would there be tears in the eyes of the audience?" The answer is usually "yes." If those tears have never been cried for you, you need to cry them for yourself. When you Tap and cry those tears, you'll be free. Having such an emotionally charged event like this that you never honor keeps it with you. Until you honor the grief, loss, and pain, it stays stuck. Now for the final time, close your eyes and see yourself in that movie again. If you received a gift from going through this event, what would it be? What did you learn that has made you more wise and savvy? What skills did you learn that you really needed? What mistakes will you never make again? What did you learn about yourself, your strength, and your willingness to work hard?

The truth is, you've already come through this event and received gifts from it that you use all the time. How do they help for this new goal? Let this goal trauma story transform into your hero story! Getting through old events can become *the* reason you do trust yourself more now and know your strengths. Think about it and ask yourself, "If I could live through that, can I handle just about anything this new goal throws my way?" Sometimes challenges are put in your path to strengthen and prepare you for what's coming next; you need to learn some lessons before you're ready to take on your true goals and be the hero of your mission. Could that be true for you?

I'll end this chapter with a truly positive round focused on your current goal so you can arouse your personal power and willingness to go after it.

TAPPING SCRIPT FOR GOAL TRAUMA, ROUND 3

Tap through all the points, using the following phrases:

As I let go of this old story *** I come back to my goal for today *** And it may seem a little crazy and impossible *** That's okay *** But the truth is *** I really do want it *** Yes, I have some fears *** Of course I do.

I am human! *** But too bad, I want it anyway *** And I am going for it *** Yes, of course I still worry about failure *** I don't want to fail *** But I really *do* want this *** And I am smarter and stronger and ready *** I am going for it.

Now! *** With all my brilliance ** All my passion *** And all my energy *** This is my time *** And this is my choice *** And I really do want this *** I may have done things the hard way in the past *** But I believe that this can and will unfold for me miraculously *** And I am now totally open *** And expecting that! *** I'm open to this goal unfolding as a miracle for me *** I'm open to this being *** An amazing, fun, exciting journey *** That will require me *** To step up with brilliance.

Inspiration *** Fearlessness *** Excitement *** And passion *** And I am up for the challenge *** I am the hero of my story *** And I now allow this goal to be my hero's journey *** Inspiring me to grow and stretch and shine! *** I declare that I do want this *** This is my dream! *** This is my life *** This is my mountain *** And I am climbing it!

Take a nice deep breath. Notice how much of your energy rose up with those words and how much more ready you feel to go after your goal! That's the end of the dark cloud of the goal trauma.

A Surprising Exercise to Claim Your Super-Hero Powers: Discover all the gifts you truly possess from past mistakes and apply what you've learned to everything you do.
www.TappingIntoWealth.com/Video11

12

"I DON'T DESERVE MORE MONEY"

I f I had to pick only one thing from this book that you should focus on if you did nothing else, it would be dealing with your worth and deserving set point. This is the chapter where the biggest changes happen. It's often the work that must be prefaced with the most explanation to convince people they need to do it.

When I say the words "worthy" and "deserving," I often get lots of resistance from people who insist, "I have no self-esteem issues. I feel worthy." And they continue, "I'm not one of *those* people with low self-esteem, so this doesn't relate to me." Then they share proof of their healthy self-esteem and confidence, pointing to educational degrees, their wealth of experience, or how successful they've been. "See, I have all the confidence in the world. This isn't my issue," they conclude. But when they look at big goals, they might confess: "I don't have a worthiness issue, I just . . .

- Am not smart enough to earn that much."
- Am not unique or special enough."

- Have a really hard time asking to be paid."
- Worry people won't like what I offer."

Do you see the contradiction in these beliefs? You've probably known people with accomplishments, education, or amazing experience who should have very high confidence and self-esteem and may appear to on the outside; yet they make choices that counter it. Smart, successful people still get into relationships with abusive, critical, or controlling partners or allow themselves to be underpaid and taken advantage of at work. Or they ignore their health and appearance. That incongruity doesn't reflect true self-esteem!

Understanding Income Set Points

My definitions of "worthy" and "deserving" are based on the idea of a set point. First, understand that beliefs about your worthiness aren't black or white. They're somewhere on a huge range of the worthiness/deserving continuum. You're wired with an inner set point indicating how worthy and deserving you are of all the money, reward, and pleasure that's possible. This inner set point acts like a preset thermostat to modulate how much you need to keep the balance at your current level of worthiness.

It doesn't matter whether you have good self-esteem or confidence, or feel worthy right now. The critical factor is what your range is. When you set an intention to go from your current level to way beyond it, you must work with your worthy and deserving set point. The goal you set earlier is way above your current level, so it's important to do inner worthiness work to match it. Otherwise, you'll find ways to sabotage your success or create some hardship with each higher level to offset the otherwise good feelings of having it.

How can you determine your worthy and deserving set point? Easy!

Just look objectively at your life. You are, right now, at the exact level of how worthy and deserving you feel in each category:

- Your income and overall wealth
- Physical health and ease
- Loving and being loved
- Success
- Relaxation time
- Reward
- Pleasure

You're always at your set point. Pay attention to anything on the list that feels woefully off balance. Even if you're happy with your life, when you set a goal and take action to push beyond where you are, you'll often feel worthiness issues arise because inside you is a programmed, finely honed, totally unconscious set point that governs the balance of your pain versus pleasure and struggle versus joy continuum, with implications on much more than just money. Your internal set point includes:

- How hard you must work for your money
- How much you should earn
- How much you should save
- How much relaxation time you're allowed
- How much reward, love, and joy you're allowed
- How much ease and pleasure in your body you're allowed

Your worthy and deserving set point governs exactly how much good you get in all aspects of your life. If one area gets out of balance, other areas may get offset to restore this inner balance. For example, if your income greatly increases beyond your current set point, you might unconsciously sabotage it and/or create ways to get rid of money. Or you might gain thirty pounds and feel bad about how you look. That's why you must address this now, since the income goal you set is about to propel you way beyond your set point and throw a huge monkey wrench into the balance. Without inner work to raise your worthy and deserving set point, it offsets the balance and triggers responses to hurt what you've achieved. You may protest that you'd never do that and insist that you do want more money. But remember, you don't commit self-sabotage consciously.

Have you or someone you know achieved a goal and then did something to foil or undermine the success? Or did you observe someone earn more money but suffer in another area of life? When you look back, the contributing factors to the negative outcome seem random, external, and unrelated. Or it might be hard to imagine how or why you'd self-sabotage. Yet it happens! A masterful part of your mind monitors whether you've gone beyond your set point. When you do, it takes over on autopilot and drives actions you take, or don't take, that you're not aware of to balance you. They pull back your success to return balance to the set point and will seem unrelated to each other. On the outside, they sound like:

- "I procrastinate."
- "I'm overwhelmed."
- "I can't decide what I should focus on first."
- "I'm foggy, overtired, exhausted."
- "I am so anxious and worried."
- "I can't trust anyone/I'm the only one who can do it."
- "I got caught up running too many errands, fulfilling obligations."
- "I don't have time to look at that/I'm overcommitted."

These are calling cards of unconscious actions that masterfully work together to maintain your worthy and deserving set point. I've watched in amazement how quickly and accurately these actions return people to their set point. What commonly offsets increased income is needing more time to do the work. Two people may do the same job for the same pay, but one works forty hours a week while the other needs sixty. There will appear to be many external reasons, circumstances, or complications that create a sixty-hour week. Clearly the two people have different set points for how hard they must work and how exhausted they need to be to deserve the reward. I see this often.

But there's an upside! Just as your unconscious actions sabotage, they can also support you. When you do the inner work to shift your set point up, all the masterful autopilot actions will be available to help your efforts! The exercises in this chapter will have you look at your outrageous income goal and get incredibly honest about how worthy and deserving you feel about earning that much money. When you do these exercises, feel what happens inside, regardless of what your mind says.

To start, here are some questions to help expose the contradictions between the level of self-esteem and worthiness you think you have and what your actions reveal. At the core of these questions is one key theme: How do you treat yourself?

- How kind and compassionate to yourself are you when you're sick? Are you allowed to rest?
- Are you allowed to relax after a long day of work without feeling guilt from not getting more done?
- Are you allowed to relax on weekends without feeling selfish or guilty if you're not helping someone, or cleaning, or somehow being productive?
- Do you sacrifice for your family or others to the point of exhaustion?
- Do you often say you'd love to get a massage, but never find time?
- How loud and ruthless is your inner critic?

Seemingly harmless, unconscious behaviors reveal your actual worthy and deserving set point. The reality is, you treat yourself in the same worthy and deserving way that your inner set point mandates. So you will withhold or allow yourself to have as much relaxation, pleasure, and relief from guilt as you feel you deserve. Another indication of your set point is having a daily debt of energy and time, meaning you never have enough time or are always exhausted. There are a million ways to convince yourself it's due to factors far beyond your control. But what if there's an internal driver creating this reality from your set point? Your inner belief in the value of your time and efforts determines how much of your time and energy must be given to feel deserving of other people's money, love, appreciation, or validation.

When you recognize your need to work extremely hard for long hours, you'll have an "aha" moment about your worthy and deserving set point. Within you, there's a belief that your efforts, intelligence, energy, efficiency, and innate value is somehow lower than it should be. It pushes you to work longer than necessary, to give more and do more in order to feel you deserve to earn more. Looking at anyone's behavior and working backward reveals the feelings and beliefs about their worthy and deserving set point.

How You Really Value You

Look back at your work in chapter 5 on your earliest money paradigm. Were your parents role models for your set point? Maybe they had to work hard for every penny, or maybe they said things like, "You've got to work harder to get ahead." Maybe they criticized people who were lazy and didn't work hard for their success or were just lucky. That message clearly says that people like that don't deserve the money and a good life. Programming from your earliest money paradigm can wreak havoc on your deserving meter. It can be hard to recognize that in many little unconscious ways, you attract more work to meet daily quotas of what you must give to feel deserving of other people's money and love, or even of your own leisure time.

"How could that possibly be?" people ask skeptically. With unconscious actions and inactions, you attract and create an amazingly complex and convoluted set of circumstances that you can point to as being out of your control; it seems like outside forces keep you stuck at your set point. This set of circumstances causes you to be less efficient with your time and less creative, inspired, and focused on strategies. You'll overdo some tasks and underdo others. Your time is always on sale. Does that sound familiar? Here are questions to help you to see more of your unconscious "I don't deserve" actions:

- Can you say "no" to people and extra responsibilities that will further tax your energy and time and complicate your life?
- Do you self-advocate for the resources *you* need to have time and energy to focus and regroup?
- Do you respect your time and ask others, including your family, to as well?

These are tough questions if your life is built on an excess of doing for others. People-pleasing says loudly, "I don't deserve!" even if it's unconscious. Opening your eyes to this behavior can be very uncomfortable. If you feel resistance to the work, take a deep breath and honor that you're trying to do something hard for a bigger payoff. Honor your inner skeptic if it shouts to distract you. Remember that you're doing what 95 percent of people never do—looking with bold honesty at yourself and your unconscious behavior so you can rise to the next level. You're not doing this because you have to, or need therapy, or have "Charlie Sheened" your life. It's because you want to make a quantum leap in your money, success, and pleasure. It's because you have an inner drive and desire to step into the bigger, bolder, more alive, and well-paid version of you!

Now observe: Do you pat yourself on the back for the million things you do well? How often does your inner self-talk say, "I should've done more, or better, or tried harder." Compare that to how often your inner voice sounds like a proud cheerleader, "*Wow!* I nailed that and am so proud of myself!" It's enlightening to pay attention to your inner, private reinforcement of your worthy and deserving set point—a *huge* indicator of how you treat yourself. You berate and criticize yourself exactly as much as you feel you deserve. Likewise, you'll be as kind and supportive as you feel you deserve.

A common question about the worthy and deserving set point is how it works with the Law of Attraction. When people say, "The Law of Attraction doesn't work for me," it usually means that the set point is a factor. The Law of Attraction teaches that you should ask for what you want. But even if you're in harmony about wanting your goal and can visualize it, the worthy/deserving set point acts as an inner pushback against it, as if part of you shouts, "I'm comfortable where I am." This waters down desires, since you're not completely aligned with wanting it, so it interferes with manifesting what you want.

GUILT AND YOUR SET POINT
We're programmed, particularly from early school experiences, to feel guilt and shame because of our mistakes. But think about how many tasks you do well every day while berating yourself for one thing you missed. This is a big unconscious habit that limits you—one you must break! Pay attention. Guilt is a key warning bell that's triggered when you've pushed past your current worthy/deserving set point. When you start to receive more, whether it's money, pleasure, reward, recognition, or even just a day of relaxation, and it goes beyond your set point, you'll experience guilt, and often feel selfish. These are alarms hardwired to alert you that you've exceeded your set point. People are willing to talk about feeling guilty for stuff but don't connect that with the worthy

and deserving issue. They say, "I don't have a self-worth issue. I just feel guilty relaxing."

Here's the "aha" moment: What do you do when you feel guilty or selfish? People have two general reactions. Probably the most common is to rapidly spring into action with all of your habitual behavior to offset those feelings. These are the "over-reactions": overdoing, overgiving, overworking, overeating, and the like. Many overgift—spend too much on people to ease the guilt of not doing enough for them. You may spend money earmarked for something important or incur more credit card debt, but, *whew*, the guilt leaves! By the time you're done with knee-jerk, guilt-reducing actions, you have a debt of energy, resources, and time, and are worn out.

The second reaction is rebellion that turns into guilt and/or self-sabotage. For example, you finally do something for yourself. As you enjoy it, guilt hits. It's often triggered by a judgmental comment from someone else like, "Wow, it must be nice to be you." They may even follow that comment by telling you how they're way too busy or responsible to get to enjoy that, reminding you to feel guilty and selfish. For some, this also triggers anger and resentment, which gives you permission to rebel and battle with other people and your own inner voice that attempts to impose the come-back-to-your-set-point guilt.

Unfortunately, when you're in rebel and battle mode, you spring into "I'll show you!" behavior—other overreactions: you'll overindulge, overspend, overrelax, and overparty while being very defensive. In this mode you're likely to go into battle with key people and resources that you need for success and happiness. As the destruction piles up, you'll eventually swing back to guilt and a healthy dose of shame. Then the cycle of overdoing returns to bring you back to your set point. Sometimes the shame from the mess you made in rebel mode proves you should lower your worthy and deserving set point. This is how people go into a downward cycle and hit rock bottom.

Look at your life. How much time do you spend feeling guilty or trying to prove you're not selfish or trying to avoid feeling more guilt? Take a hard look at how much that determines your behavior. Guilt and feeling selfish are foot soldiers in the inner battle to constantly reset the balance of pain/pleasure and struggle/joy when you've gone past your set point. From this moment on, please remember that when you feel guilt, you actually mean "I don't deserve" whatever reward or pleasure you're experiencing. Guilt says, "You don't deserve this reward, this money, this recognition, this relaxation." It's one of the most powerful drivers of behavior and will always prevail unless you start seeing, challenging, and releasing it.

RAISING YOUR SET POINT

How can you increase your worthy and deserving set point? First, begin to build up your value and unique talents and gifts in *your* own heart, mind, and belief system. This is totally an inside job. You must find and challenge all your worthy and deserving negative beliefs and rewrite the old programming with a powerful new recognition and belief in yourself—your contributions, potential, value, and the value of your time and energy. Tapping works well to clear it!

Second, increase the value of your time and contributions by Tapping into more of your own brilliance, creativity, inspired actions, and leadership. It's important to know that this happens naturally as you start to clear away negative beliefs, but can be enhanced exponentially with a simple technique—consciously ask yourself for more of your own brilliance to surface. Directly ask your inner potential for more inspirations, inspired actions, energy, leadership, courage, or whatever is needed for your goal. When you ask, it appears! Believe that you have more untapped potential and brilliance than you can imagine just waiting to be accessed.

~ *Believe you have it in you, ask for it and it will appear.* ~

When you start to experience and observe yourself operating with more of your great attributes, your worthy and deserving set point will consciously rise. This is the upward spiral of increasing brilliance, confidence, and reward. Start to identify and clarify what negative beliefs come up as you look at blasting past your current set point so you can clear them with Tapping. Use the big income goal you set for the next exercise.

Exercise for Deserving

Look at your income goal and write these sentences:

- *"I totally deserve to earn $_____" (fill in the amount of your goal).*
- *"My gifts and talents are valuable enough to earn $_____."*

Say these sentences out loud and notice how you feel inside. How true does it feel on a scale of 1 to 10? I'm not asking how true you want it to be, but how true it really feels, down in your gut. Note the numbers and push your set point even harder by adding how much time you plan to work per week to earn that much. Repeat the sentences:

- *"I totally deserve to earn $_____ working _____ hours a week."*
- *"My gifts and talents are valuable enough to earn $_____ in _____ hours a week."*

How true does it feel on a scale of 1 to 10? What beliefs or feelings pop up from saying these things aloud? Do you feel competing beliefs about your innate worth and the value of your time, energy, and brilliance?

This is eye-opening for most people because you wouldn't normally say something like that and measure your feelings after. Now take this further and shine a spotlight with your imagination on any feelings of guilt, shame, embarrassment, and judgment about what's selfish and drives your set point.

Close your eyes and visualize your income goal on a gigantic sign you're holding over your head on a stage, in front of thousands of people—everyone you know: parents (even if they passed away), siblings, other family members, friends, colleagues, current and potential customers or clients, people from school, all your teachers, and the like. As they watch you holding the sign, declare two things very loudly.

First, imagine yourself saying, "This is what I want to earn and I deserve it!" Keep your eyes closed and note your feelings. Is there embarrassment, shame, or fear? Imagining the audience, what reaction do you visualize? Shock and skepticism, or are they cheering? Pay attention to the vision. Your unconscious mind is painting a powerful and telling picture filled with insights about your set point. You're projecting your inner battle with your greatness on the audience's reactions.

Next say, "I can do it!" What feelings does that evoke, and what's the audience's reaction? You're starting to see all resistance and pushback that blocks really going after this goal.

If you don't feel completely worthy and deserving of this number, unconscious actions will eventually kick in and sabotage your progress. Add one more aspect into this picture: imagine declaring how many hours you'd like to work for that money, and be honest. You might want to work twenty hours a week, but saying it on this imaginary stage can feel awkward. When you're already working forty-plus hours, limiting beliefs about how hard you need to work to double or triple your income will double or triple. That's why it's so important to include the time. It triggers more stuff to clear so you don't offset earning more money by unconsciously creating work that requires longer hours.

Take a minute to write down whatever you feel, see, and experience in your body and mind from the visualization. There's a treasure trove of great information to be gleaned in this process that clearly illuminates the most important blocks to realizing this goal and transforming your current finances into a new wealth reality. The Tapping script below is intended to clear things that may have arisen from these exercises. Adapt it to the words, experiences, and feelings you relate to the most. When you do the visualization, *your* inner critic is automatically projected onto the audience. Did you see some supportive people and some skeptics? Or just naysayers asking, "How dare you?!"

I have done this exercise with thousands of people, and many have shared with me that the audience laughed or shunned them or actually got angry and abusive. By revealing your fears and expectations about being judged harshly, this inner projection highlights your own questions about whether or not you are worthy of the next level of success and wealth. They are important to clarify because once you see them, you can rapidly and effectively eliminate them with Tapping. That ends massive amounts of procrastination—and sabotage. Then use Tapping to start opening up and asking for higher levels of your own great attributes to take over. This is the most powerful, life-changing work you can do to create your life from within.

It's not easy to look honestly at some of the issues you've carried for a lifetime, and it takes courage and a willingness to clear these beliefs. But doing this results in *you* becoming the alive, charged, and brilliant you, and getting paid well for it. The Tapping scripts below will first deal with negative beliefs that push back against very big goals. To use the scripts most powerfully, voice the negatives as loudly and often as possible, in an over-the-top manner, to break the cycle much more quickly. Use the words in the script a few times before using your own. If they feel overexaggerated for your situation, voice them anyway. They won't instill any negative beliefs. When you say a negative phrase loudly, it feels less true and important because it's released.

This Tapping is designed to reflect and clear some of your most negative programming, which makes it the most negative sounding to start. To prepare, tune in to your goal and all your reactions to the sentences and visualizations above. Feel the resistance, emotions, and limiting beliefs.

TAPPING SCRIPT FOR YOUR WORTHY AND DESERVING SET POINT

Say the following phrases aloud while Tapping through all the points:

I really do want to earn that much money *** But that process was really eye-opening *** I really felt my resistance *** There is a part of me *** Pushing back *** That is not really sure that I deserve to make that much money *** There's an inner skeptic in me *** That truly questions my worth and value.

There's a part of me *** That strongly resists declaring I deserve this *** I can feel this part of me pushing back *** Arguing with me *** Insisting that I don't deserve to earn that much money *** Especially by working so few hours *** This part of me says that it's selfish *** And wrong for me to even ask *** To earn that much money.

*** When I said I deserve it *** I immediately felt some guilt *** Some fear *** Some shame *** When I visualized the crowd of people *** It felt embarrassing *** Who do I think I am?

Do I really think that I'm that special? *** Part of me says I'm not that special *** I'm not that unique *** People will not pay me that much money *** And there's nothing I could possibly do to earn that much *** Unless I worked a million hours *** I'm not special enough *** Brilliant enough *** Talented enough *** I am just not good enough *** This loud and clear voice *** That pushes back against my goal *** The voice that keeps me in check *** I hear that really loudly *** And it's got some pretty nasty things to say *** Who do I think I am to say I deserve that much money?

On some level it feels selfish *** And wrong *** And I feel ashamed *** Embarrassed *** And guilty *** And I have this expectation that if anyone else knew *** They would agree that I'm not good enough *** That asking for that much money is wrong.

It's arrogant! *** There's nothing that is special enough about me *** That makes me deserve that much money *** I'm just going to honor all of this *** I'm seeing and feeling my inner worthy and deserving set point *** I'm seeing and feeling the unconscious discomfort *** I want to step beyond my set point *** I'm seeing and feeling the hidden drivers *** That will cause me to sabotage *** Or create struggle and suffering *** To keep me at my set point *** I am seeing and feeling *** What is really driving my unconscious behaviors *** All the autopilot behaviors *** That keep me stuck *** I'm just going to honor it.

Take a nice deep breath. I encourage you to repeat that round and go deeper and longer on any parts that resonate with you. Continue to voice as loudly as possible any negative emotions or self-talk that surface while Tapping, and they will subside. Now redo the above sentence exercises and rate your feelings from 1 to 10. As you'll see, Tapping can dramatically shift your feelings of worthiness and value related to your goal. That's a huge boost in your worthy and deserving set point!

Now you can proactively increase your set point. Clearing limiting beliefs often brings a new level of perspective and appreciation for your unique value and talents. You already have a storehouse of untapped potential brilliance and energy that's far beyond what you've seen so far. Your negative programming limited its use, but it's time to change that! The key to taking your worthy and deserving set point high enough to match how much money you want, in how many hours, is to start bursting with more of your own unique abilities.

Ask yourself to reveal more of your untapped resources. Something amazing will spring out of you, assuming your negative programming and beliefs don't beat it down with ruthless criticism. When it appears, pat yourself on the back and yell, "I rock!" Then you'll live in the upward spiral of your worthy and deserving set point! I'll end this chapter with a round of Tapping into more of your brilliance.

TAPPING SCRIPT FOR MORE OF YOUR BRILLIANCE

Say the following phrases aloud while Tapping on the karate chop point:

Even though part of me does not believe I am really worthy and deserving of this goal of earning this much money, by working this many hours, and all the joy, pleasure, and ease that will be in my life as a result, I'm just going to honor and observe that for now.

Even though part of me really questions whether or not I have the brilliance, the talent, the gifts, or the energy to earn this much money in this much time, I recognize I've never earned that much before. And it's hard to imagine, but the truth is, there is more to me than I've seen so far. Buried within me is an untapped resource of brilliance, of boundless energy, of courage and enthusiasm, of inspiration and focus, and efficient actions.

Say the following phrases aloud while Tapping into all the points:

I have an untapped potential within me *** I have untapped genius *** I may have seen some so far in my life *** But that is nothing *** Compared to how much more *** I can unleash *** So I am now asking for more *** Of my own brilliance to appear *** I am now allowing more inspiration *** To flow through me *** I am ready for streamlined *** Efficient actions to manifest *** Through my very hands.

I speak directly to my subconscious mind *** The part of me that makes quantum leaps *** That is creative *** That has million-dollar ideas *** Just waiting to come forward *** And I ask this part of me *** For more brilliant ideas *** For inspirations *** For courage *** For audacious action *** For higher levels of leadership to emerge *** For leveraged and efficient strategies to appear *** I ask this of my unconscious mind.

Knowing it is a treasury of untapped brilliance *** And I'm open and ready *** And accepting and willing *** For all the ideas, the inspirations *** And nudges to act and appear *** And when they do, I commit to hearing them *** With an open mind and open heart *** I commit to taking action *** And recognizing the signs of my own brilliant genius *** I believe that there is more to me *** Than what I have seen so far *** Than what I have shown so far *** And I'm open and allowing my brilliant genius to come through *** For my highest good.

Take a nice deep breath. Do this round a few times until you feel better about how worthy and deserving you are. Once you raise your set point, money will come to you more easily.

Getting Real and Getting Over the Inner Value Battle: Uncover why you doubt yourself and your value when it matters most, and how you can shift to a consistently empowered state.
www.TappingIntoWealth.com/Video12

13

· ———— ·

BREAKING THE CYCLE OF
ALWAYS STRIVING
BUT NEVER ARRIVING

Why don't I have more money?" Do you feel like you work hard but never get to the level of reward you desire in terms of money, credibility, position, or ease? Do you see other people doing the same work as you, maybe not even as well, but getting seen, validated, and handsomely rewarded for their efforts? It can be frustrating when you strive and strive and strive to make more money and reach a level of success, but the day of reaping the bigger rewards of your hard work never seems to arrive. I'll address that pattern in this chapter. It's time for you to:

- Take the work you've put into your struggling new business and create a fabulously successful company
- Reveal all the brilliance, experience, and expertise you possess, and be valued in your industry by colleagues, bosses, or customers
- Reap the benefits of the long hours you put into your work so you can rise to the top of your profession
- Create multiple streams of income

Perfection

There's another negative vow that greatly sabotages and limits your ability to accumulate wealth. This vow applies to you if you're the type who likes to achieve and hold yourself and others to a very high standard. You'll also relate more if you're one of those people who loves to learn or master everything you can get your hands on, or if you truly are an expert at what you do. It actually applies to anyone who holds a very, very high standard of perfection—the vow to be perfect. Often with little prodding, people know right away, "Oh, this is my issue."

It's a common lesson in the self-development world that people shouldn't strive to be perfect, that there's no such thing as perfection, that it's bad to be a perfectionist. Yet many people still operate with an inner belief that if they try harder to be better—the best, perfect— then everything will be so much better in all areas of their lives. So many take a vow: "I have to be perfect and will be critical of myself until I am." They don't see perfectionism as a problem. In their minds, they think, "It makes sense for me to have this vow. It works for me."

This vow can be seen in two ways through the inner critic. When you look at a mistake from your past—for example, a "financial trauma" as was discussed in chapter 6—the vow to be perfect means the mistake you made was and is unforgivable. You look back at the event with the belief that "I should have known better." And you feel at fault, believing that you deserve "the punishment" or loss that you experienced. As I said in previous chapters, Tapping can clear this kind of belief.

The second aspect of this vow, which we'll focus on in this chapter, is how you may look back at an accomplishment from the past that went well, but still think, "I could have done it even better." The vow of perfection means your inner critic only sees all the things you missed and all the ways you fell short of your inner standard of perfection. So from that point of view, you'll always feel that you don't quite deserve money, reward, and credibility—*yet*—because you're not perfect yet. Since there's always room for improvement, you can always justify your self-criticism with logic. That makes it harder to clear out this vow. It may seem logical to try to do everything perfectly, but there's a huge downside to having a vow to be perfect. When you live by that vow, you tell the universe:

- "I'm not perfect yet, so I don't deserve the rewards of what I'm doing until I get it right."
- "I don't deserve the attention and praise. I don't deserve the compensation. I don't deserve the respect, the credibility."

Since achieving perfection is impossible, vowing to be perfect means you'll always strive but never arrive at a point that satisfies you enough to believe you deserve large financial rewards. In addition, every goal you set and every action you take toward that goal will have the added pressure that everything must be done perfectly. When you don't achieve that, you'll suffer the internal barrage of "I could have been better" and an endless review of each mistake.

Have you ever worked for someone or had a parent who could never be fully pleased because nothing was ever good enough, or measured up to his or her impossible standards? It's a demoralizing environment that creates self-doubt and anxiety around taking action. Your inner vow of perfection will create the same fear and constant second-guessing that immobilizes many brilliant people from either getting started or finishing what they start. I believe this vow keeps many people stuck, and prevents them from taking all kinds of action that would benefit their careers, including creating products, writing books, giving talks, and marketing themselves. Instead, they busy themselves with smaller tasks and actions that they can execute perfectly and talk about being "ready someday" to do more.

One of the most effective ways to detect if you have this vow is to do this exercise:

Exercise for the Negative Vow of Perfection

Think about the last thing that you accomplished. As you recall it, does your mind go to some version of "I just know I could have done better"? Or "I should've done more"? Or "Why didn't I prepare more?" Do those kinds of thoughts have stronger power than thoughts of how well you did?

Having any of those kinds of thoughts is a classic telltale sign of a vow to be perfect. And there's no compassion in how you perceive yourself as imperfect. When you've taken a vow to be perfect, you tend to be very, very ruthless with yourself. Your inner critic goes to town, looking for what it can find wrong. Even if you work hard and do something well, it still says, "No, you could've been better," which again means, "You're not perfect yet." That leads you to believe, at least subconsciously, "I don't actually deserve yet. I have to wait until I do better." Or it may mean, "Hey, universe—I deserve exactly what I'm getting in these mediocre results, this mediocre pay, this mediocre credibility in my field, because I don't deserve more yet."

Arriving at that imagined moment when perfection is finally achieved is always elusive, so you'll never actually claim that you're good enough to get the money you want. For example, I had a client named Julie who had a major issue with this vow. She tried a lot of self-development work but couldn't figure out what held her back from making the kind of money from her business that she should. Julie is a publicist with her own PR firm. She was full of passion for helping her clients get the media coverage they needed and advised them on how to put themselves out in the public and get positive attention to help advance their careers. Yet she wasn't able to do it for herself. When she came to me, she was very frustrated about her inability to build her business way beyond just making ends meet. After asking her the questions above, I pointed out that she'd taken a vow to be perfect and perfectly critical of herself.

Julie was stunned because she thought of herself as self-evolved. But her vow was buried deep inside her. Outwardly, she seemed to have great self-esteem and confidence. But her inner critic kept her stuck. This "aha" moment shook her up at first. Then she laughed when she acknowledged that being perfect and perfectly critical of herself fit her perfectly. She recognized that, for most of her life, she'd been shackled by her vow to be perfect, beating herself up for every imperfection. Looking back, she remembered how her parents pushed her to do everything perfectly. An A- in a class was never good enough. They pushed her to get perfect grades in school, watch her weight, have perfect manners, and basically be the perfect daughter. She was admonished any time she fell even a bit short of their high expectations.

Julie's harsh self-judgment kept her from making a big effort to market herself as a great publicist, since deep inside she didn't believe she was, even with all the positive testimonials she got. Whenever she considered approaching a bigger potential client, her vow held her back, making her feel she wasn't good enough to do the job he'd expect. She kept waiting to learn more, make more contacts, and get better at writing press releases and talking on the phone. She never felt like she knew enough. While seeking perfection had plagued her since childhood, Julie didn't notice this pattern until we spoke and she saw all the ways she worked hard with just mediocre financial rewards.

She finally recognized how she could never tap into her passion for the work she loved. It was almost as if when she got close to getting to the next level of her career, her inner critic stepped in to block it. Just as a positive door opened, Julie's fear of not being perfect made her shut it fast. She didn't return calls from media people because she was scared of saying the wrong thing. She referred potential clients with higher profiles (and more money) than she was used to representing to other publicists. She was afraid she couldn't handle them well. Julie even passed on an opportunity to partner with someone more successful because her inner critic made sure she felt too inferior to do so. She worried that the woman might be disappointed in her ability and couldn't risk that.

When Julie came to me, she'd just been referred to the CEO of a large company who was interested in her doing publicity for his new launch. Tired of losing opportunities, she asked for help getting out of her own way. She was unaware of the vow that she had made to be perfect until we spoke, but she knew that something was holding her back. Clearing that block made a huge shift in her business and her life in general. Julie's big "aha" was accepting how her constantly critical mind kept her stuck in a mental prison because of her perceived inadequacies.

In her quest to not look stupid and in feeling like she wasn't a good enough publicist, Julie created invisible bars that kept her locked into beliefs that she needed more experience before she could put herself and her business out there more. While on an intellectual level she knew her clients were very satisfied and she'd developed solid relationships with the media, her subconscious childhood belief that she always needed to get an A+ made her feel she had to strive more before she was worthy of increasing her business and her wealth. Julie was so afraid to fail, that she could never own herself as the good publicist she is. That kept her from taking risks and trusting that she offered her clients an excellent service.

Tapping on her need for perfection gave Julie clarity about why, with all the striving she did, she never arrived at her goals. That awareness allowed her to consciously change her thoughts about not being ready to advance her business. She knew she was! Further Tapping gave her the boost she needed to take more action. When old thoughts came up, she Tapped on them and was able to move forward. Her income has since doubled, and her business is expanding with her confidence in her ability to do a good job for clients, even big ones. Even more exciting for her are the goals she continues to create for herself. She'd never made money goals before, since it seemed hopeless to get beyond where she was. Now Julie's vision has no limits.

Julie illustrates the connection between the vow to be perfect and the inner critic that comes with it. She took the vow to be perfectly critical of herself until she reached that perfection, which of course is unattainable. Do you see some of this vow in you? We'll use Tapping to clear away this vow to be perfect. As with some of the other blocks, you might have internal resistance to letting go of this vow because it may have been operating for you in a very strong way. As you do the Tapping, try to recognize the downside of always needing to be perfect and the upside of letting it go.

While you'll always hold yourself to a high standard and love achieving and being awesome, once the vow is cleared, it will be a choice, not a vow to be perfect. That's when you get to have fun being totally awesome and receiving the money, respect, credibility, support, and love that comes from that awesomeness. Choose to be awesome instead of having a vow that makes your inner critic run all the time. Now here's an exercise to set up a round of Tapping for the vow of perfection.

Exercise for Identifying Feelings about Being Perfect

Think about a moment from the past when you did something pretty well (maybe even great by others' standards) but you still rehash in your mind all the ways you could have and should have done it even better— even more perfectly. You probably have one. This should be an instance when you look back and think something like:

(continued)

> • *"I should've worked harder."*
> • *"I should've done better."*
> • *"I should've been smarter."*
> • *"I should have prepared more."*
> • *"I should have looked more confident."*
>
> *Those kinds of statements are telltale signs of the ruthless inner critic reminding you that nothing you ever do is quite good enough. Think about what happened to you that triggered those kinds of thoughts and say out loud, "I should have or could have done better!" On a scale of 1 to 10, how true does that feel?*

Now we'll do some Tapping specifically on that vow. In the first round, make an effort to really voice your feelings about the ruthless inner critic. Remember, your goal is to lighten it and clear it up and out of your energy system.

TAPPING SCRIPT FOR
RELEASING PERFECTION #1

Tap through all the points, using the following phrases:

There I am, I guess I did *okay* *** But it was not my best *** It was not *the* best *** I should've done better *** Should've, should've, should've *** And I am right about that *** I am always right about that *** I could have done it better *** I could have and should have *** Worked harder *** Been smarter *** Prepared more *** Been more confident *** I should be better at this by now *** I should have been perfect *** And it wasn't perfect *** I should have done better *** I should have pushed myself even harder.

Now it's too late *** Everyone saw me flawed, less than the best *** And that is unacceptable for me *** I should have been better *** And that is the truth *** No room for human mistakes *** No room for compassion *** I deserve this indictment *** Just not good enough *** I have a very high standard for myself *** And I am proud of that *** Why would I want to change that? *** I don't want to be a slacker! *** This inner critical voice is really working for me.

Take a nice deep breath, then look back at the story right now and say, "I should've done better," or "I should have been perfect." See how intense those statements feel to you now. Of course it's true that you could have done better, because there is an infinite number of ways to improve. The question is, are you feeling a more balanced perspective on the reality of how you did, versus the barrage of "I am not good enough/could have been better"?

This vow may take more Tapping rounds to break because it's not a real feeling, which can be more easily Tapped on. This is a pattern of thinking that has been operating for a long time and will feel both true and justified. It's the very dark side of your inner calling to excellence, mastery, and achieving at a personal high standard. Out of balance, this becomes the eye always searching for mistakes and shortcomings and the voice of unending criticism. Because of this, there's a sort of pride and righteousness attached to this inner talk that make it trickier to clear.

So, if your inner critic still says, "Yes—but . . . it could have been better" rewind the tape and tap through it again. The more you Tap on it, the more you'll start to feel a lessening of the rigid view of what "perfection" you've been striving for and an appreciation for what you did achieve. After doing this first round of Tapping, you might think about your story and suddenly feel respect for what you did accomplish and what you learned. Now look at that story and say, "I did great!" When you can say that and really mean it, you have shifted your vibe to one of receiving and deserving *now*, not when you eventually become some image of perfection.

Do you look at that event and feel the enthusiasm to be better, push harder, and achieve more? That's great if it comes from a mind-set of "I am awesome and I choose to keep rising up to *higher levels* instead of *never feeling good enough*." You should have a belief that honors how much you deserve reward, validation, and credibility—right now, not when you earn it through perfection. Your view should bring energy, enthusiasm, and self-value into the next thing you do. Thinking with the other mind-set is like saying loudly, "I don't deserve yet!" and it brings criticism, fear, and self-recrimination into the next thing you do. Which sounds better to you?

I want you to really feel the difference between striving for perfection and trying to do your best so you can choose the latter. If you aren't there yet, rewind the video and Tap through that critical mind-set again until you get some shift in your thinking on this. There's a connection between the vow to be perfect and what you allow yourself to receive. Breaking this vow changes what you declare, energetically, that you deserve. Once the intensity of the last round has lowered, do a positive round that allows you to be both a person who loves to strive for excellence and mastery, but knows that you deserve amazing rewards right now. And you accept that perfection is an ever-changing target. Here's another round of Tapping to reinforce the positives:

TAPPING SCRIPT FOR
RELEASING PERFECTION #2

Tap through all the points, using the following phrases:

There I was *** I am open to seeing I did pretty good *** I did better than most would have *** Yes, you can always improve *** And I do love being the best *** But I never really let myself *** Celebrate when I do great *** I downplay it *** Why would I celebrate? *** There is time for that when I am perfect *** Wow, that is pretty harsh *** Because there is no perfect *** I just stay stuck striving for it *** And never get to celebrate *** Feel complete *** And allow myself to be rewarded for my awesomeness *** I honor myself now.

I actually did the best I knew how at the time *** I actually did great *** I'm open to giving myself that gift *** And feeling my deserving at a deep level *** I totally honor that I've always been doing my best *** I've never *not* deserved *** I honor my deserving right now *** Even before I lift another finger and achieve another thing *** I deserve right now *** I'm opening my heart to my own deserving *** Of course I deserve *** I deserve love, money, attention *** Deserve wealth, security.

I deserve to be seen as the expert I am *** I deserve to have a blast being awesome *** Because it's fun to be awesome *** I'm now forgiving and releasing this vow of perfection *** I've paid the price for it for too long *** And I'm now open to healing it *** So I can have fun being awesome *** Striving to reach my high standards *** For the joy of mastery and achievement *** Because that is the way I roll *** I do deserve to honor this *** I am so proud of myself and how much I deserve right now.

Take a nice deep breath and just notice how you feel after doing that Tapping round. Often, people experience a strong sense of both freedom and excitement to create and take action. Truly, freedom from the vow to be perfect is a gift that allows your creativity to flourish! When the desire to be great at what you do comes purely from a true impulse for mastery, without the rigid rules of perfection attached to it, your energy and focus will soar.

Sometimes people can also have a flood of tears, especially when they break the belief "It's never good enough." If you have a flood of emotions or tears, that's great. Just keep Tapping. The intensity will gradually lessen and turn to the excitement of what you can create and allow yourself to receive in return. I've heard from countless people that almost immediately after completing this exercise, others around them—colleagues, bosses, and clients—suddenly voiced respect, appreciation, and validation of their excellence.

I see this surprising turn of events as a mirror reflection of the new level at which you respect, appreciate, and validate your own excellence. Remember, you're far from the only one out there stuck striving to keep this vow to be perfect. Now you can join the many thousands who have gotten to the other side of it and started executing and creating, full of the joy and freedom to be creative. That feels so much better than waiting for the perfection that never comes before you challenge yourself, make a big move, and begin to execute steps to greatly increase your wealth.

Being Perfect Is Boring—BE AWESOME Instead: A quick way to shift out of your inner critic to be empowered and have fun
www.TappingIntoWealth.com/Video13

14

FEELING INVISIBLE

There's another very common vow that will stop you in your tracks as you go for your new goal. It hinders scores of people from going for the bigger, bolder action that's necessary to create more income and wealth. It will also certainly cause inner conflict around honoring your value, offering your services at a higher price, and setting healthy boundaries, especially when it comes to marketing yourself. Instead of owning all of your special attributes, you vow to keep your true self invisible, and the persona you show the world is someone else—someone more appropriate, acceptable, modest, self-sacrificing, and the like. You vow to be a person whom others—your family, parents, teachers, friends—have told you to be or need you to be.

Sometimes you may have taken this vow because your physical safety was at stake and you learned that if you became "invisible," you felt more secure. Having a low profile may have helped keep you off the radar screen of someone who scared you. Some people take this vow because they perceive there would be an emotional or psychological danger in the form of criticism or negativity if their true desires, feelings, or talents were revealed. Being the kind of person who gets less noticed in negative ways may seem like a safer choice. Having a persona that's low key can limit the attention given to you. So you vow to be as invisible as you can be.

The important thing to know is that regardless of where this tendency toward invisibility started, trying to reach the higher level of action, confidence, and visibility required to go after a big goal will trigger this vow. When faced with new challenges and opportunities, you'll suddenly feel very uncomfortable in two very specific ways. First, when you start to take, or even think about taking a higher level of action that means you'll become more visible, extreme fear and anxiety will be activated inside you. Second, when you speak of yourself, your value, and your goal with confidence (or even imagine speaking that way), a feeling of "I am being arrogant" will also trigger shame about it.

These are awful feelings that will stop you from taking action, since it's what they're designed to do. Autonomic nervous system reactions are great deterrents, keeping you in line with your vow to stay small, invisible, and not shine too brightly. They create a special brand of inertia and procrastination that are difficult to overcome when they're not understood. This is why it's imperative now to clearly see and feel if you've taken this vow so you can use the exercises and Tapping scripts below to eliminate it. Reaching your big goal depends on it! After you work on this vow, your willingness and courage to take bold action will soar.

It's also important to recognize how this vow already impacts your life and actions. For instance, the vow to be invisible can keep you from speaking up for and speaking well of yourself and your value. Instead, you may often downplay your worth, brush off compliments, and deflect attention and focus off yourself and onto other people. This vow

keeps the most amazing and talented people from marketing themselves in a bigger way due to a fear of public speaking. While I agree
that modesty is a much nicer trait than narcissism, there's a downside
to always having to downplay your assets and achievements in every
circumstance because it's dictated by a vow. Of course you may be ap-
preciated as a very nice, humble, and "salt of the earth" person. But,
you won't be seen as a leader in your field or a go-to person up for a
challenge.

When you subconsciously have this vow to be invisible, other people
will overlook and forget you when opportunities come up. They will
treat you as if you're invisible, which in a sense you are—in a world
where people who speak up and make themselves visible get more. The
vow to be invisible profoundly influences how you present yourself to
everyone because it reflects on your confidence, or lack thereof. Unwillingness to speak about what a valuable person you are, whether in words
or actions, comes across as having a lack of confidence about how worthy you are as a person or as an asset to your company or potential clients. The unwillingness to shine with all your unique gifts translates to
people thinking you lack unique gifts. That's why this vow can no longer exist in the same space with the new goal you've created. The vow to
be invisible will cancel out any desires or efforts to reach it.

Test Your Vow

Do you feel invisible? You might not know if the vow to be invisible is
working in your subconscious. Let's see right now if it's playing in your
life without your realizing it. Try this exercise:

EXERCISE: HOW INVISIBLE ARE YOU?

Take a nice deep breath, close your eyes, and visualize yourself standing, very nicely groomed and dressed, at the front of a room filled with at least thirty people, most of whom have some relevance or authority over your income or advancement. If you have a job in a company, fill that room with your boss, the management, and other colleagues. Include people who are dependent on you doing your job, and also people who are at least partly responsible for how much money you make or whether you get a raise and how much that raise would be.

If you're self-employed or own a small business, fill this room with your target market, so everybody there is a perfect client or anyone else who could offer a good opportunity for you. As you stand there facing them, imagine yourself saying, "I am awesome at what I do. I am a rock star at what I do. I totally deserve to be paid well for this."

Did you have an "ouch" moment, just thinking about saying that to those people? It's a common reaction. I've done this with thousands of people, and this exercise is one that greatly triggers people because most of us have, at least on some level, made the vow to be invisible. This vow motivates you to keep your true self, unique talents, and special gifts invisible. It drives you to:

- Project yourself to be someone whom you assume is more appropriate to fit in
- Reflect what other people want you to be
- Make an effort to please people and keep everyone else happy
- Be modest about your value because you believe people will like you more if you do

What I hear from people after this exercise is, "Oh, my goodness, get me out of here. I want to run out of the room." People have said, "Margaret, it just felt like I slid onto the floor and I'm in a ball and can't even deal with this exercise. It's too embarrassing and terrifying." What was your reaction? Were you comfortable with the idea of announcing how fabulous you are to everyone in that room? Think about your reaction. If it was in any way negative, we'll do some Tapping soon to clear away any intensity and programming around this vow to be invisible. Since it can affect your income, it's time to end it!

If you can't stand there fully in your own power and declare to everyone who's listening that you have tremendous value and deserve to get the money that's commensurate with that value, consider that you may have made the vow to be invisible. You may write it off as just being shy or attribute it to an upbringing that taught you that people will like you more if you don't toot your own horn and if you do your best to be modest. But when this is reinforced by a vow to be invisible, it can be the biggest roadblock to career advancement and keep your confidence low.

For example, my client Michael had a major "aha" moment around this vow and how it was running so much of his life. He worked in a large firm with many opportunities for advancement, but was always passed over when good ones opened up. For years he focused on supporting his family and trying to make their lives better. He did his job so he'd have a job but felt the work wasn't nearly on the level he was capable of. Yet he made no move to get promoted to a position he'd enjoy more, because he didn't want to rock the boat and risk losing the one he had. So he just focused on doing what he believed he was supposed to be doing and suppressed the dissatisfaction with his work.

When Michael was young, his father taught him the importance of being responsible. His definition of "responsible" meant *doing what was expected of you, keeping a low profile while doing a good job, not doing anything to annoy people, and not asking for too much; being grateful for what you have.* Michael worked hard in school and tried to do what teachers expected of him. He married his college girlfriend with the blessing of both sets of parents. He had a decent job that didn't challenge him but covered the rent, as well as some extras for his family. He stifled thoughts of "Is this all there is to life? Going to a job that bores me and being a good husband and father?" He loved his family but felt like there was nothing in his life just for him.

As we spoke, Michael's vow to be invisible—to be someone who's doing what others consider appropriate or following the "supposed to be" route—and not stand out as special became very clear. He was living in survival mode, making just enough money to support his family, with nothing satisfying for him. His time was spent being bored at work and doing things for family members. He never paid attention to his own desires, believing that as the man of his house, he was supposed to be responsible for being their provider. Other people dictated his life choices, which came from a sense of obligation and his vow, not from a place of passion, joy, or freedom.

Michael felt like he was living in a box, and everything in his life had to fit into it properly or he got uncomfortable. Speaking up for himself or actively going after a more stimulating position didn't fit into that box. Nor did thinking about activities he'd love to try on his own. Life in the box was rigid and very structured. I asked Michael if he was happy. He laughed and asked me to define "happy." He'd lost sight of enjoying life in exchange for "doing the right thing," like his father had done. Michael wanted to break out of his box and make a lot more money so he'd have freedom to live more passionately. And he wanted to make money doing something that stimulated him to use his brain and other talents.

No one at his job had the slightest idea of what Michael was capable of doing. Even when he helped others with projects, he never took credit. Yet inside he had a lot of negative emotions about not getting noticed for higher positions. While he was very smart and had better skills than most of the senior people working at his company, only Michael knew it, since he followed what he'd been taught: *Be modest; build up those you work with; don't call a lot of attention to yourself.* He said he felt stuck in his box. When he recognized that the box had been built in response to his vow to be invisible, he was shocked. He just thought it was the way it was supposed to be. But it's not.

We create boxes and shields and façades that protect us from people seeing too much of who we are. If you don't know what kind of reaction you might get if you share how great you are with others, that unknown can keep you silent. Some people who've taken a vow to be invisible call it being low key, which really means staying under people's radar by choice. Yet opportunities come most readily to those who stand out. Michael's ability to rise up to a better job and pursue his deepest desires was suppressed for the many years he lived in his invisible box. Even when he recognized his vow to be invisible, he didn't know how to end it.

After deeply connecting with feelings about how it held him back and recognizing that he didn't like this vow, Michael was able to loosen its grip by using Tapping. When you look at a picture like this, and it's full of fear and anxiety, you'll clearly see you have been programmed to feel it would be inappropriate or scary to stand there and shine with your true gifts. That absolutely blocks your ability to manifest the kind of money you want and deserve. If you relate in any way to this vow, Tap along to the following script now, using your own personal words when it's appropriate. As you Tap through the points, tune back in to that picture of you standing in front of that room full of business people. This script uses words that I commonly hear.

TAPPING SCRIPT FOR INVISIBILITY

Tap through all the points, using the following phrases:

Oh, my God, this is terrifying *** I've got to get out of this room *** So scary *** So vulnerable right now *** I want to just disappear *** I am feeling my vow to stay invisible *** I can't say, "I'm awesome at what I do" *** I can't say that out loud.

I'm just medium *** That's what I want people to hear *** Because I can see it all *** They're judging me *** They're looking at me skeptically *** They're shocked and offended that I've said this *** They're definitely judging me *** Wondering if I'm good enough *** "Who does she think she is?" *** Oh, I want to run and hide *** I don't want to be this vulnerable *** I feel very vulnerable right now *** This is really scary *** I would never say something like that *** It's not right.

I have a rule about that *** It's just not appropriate *** I made a vow never to shine this brightly *** Never to be seen like this *** I believe I have great talents and unique abilities *** But I don't want to say that out loud *** I don't want to share that with people *** They'll judge me *** They'll reject me *** They will be skeptical of my abilities *** This is all too scary *** I feel my vow to stay invisible *** Because I want to disappear right now.

Now take a nice deep breath. Look at the picture again and notice how just after voicing that and Tapping through that round, you've calmed the picture down. Also, look at the audience that you visualized at the beginning of the chapter. Often, they've shifted also, to what seems to be a less judgmental attitude and a more open and receptive approach to what you offer. If this still feels very intense and you haven't stopped wanting to run out of that room, it's okay. Rewind this video and Tap through it again. Each time you do, you turn down the fight-or-flight response in your body that's connected to this vow and this picture. The more you Tap, the calmer it gets.

When you Tap on the vow as you just did, all sorts of feelings can come up in your body. It can almost feel like a piece of you is leaving, and it can create mixed feelings about letting this vow go since you've probably had it for a long time. You may feel very uncomfortable at first. But it will free up a tremendous amount of physical energy once you let it go. You can make that happen by doing the rounds of Tapping. There will come a point when you recognize that you're unique and good at what you do. Your whole personality can benefit the people around you once you free yourself from the restraints you've lived with.

If you don't let go of this vow, people will never ever recognize how special you are. If you can't shine with your true gifts, you'll get much less than what you deserve because of a law in the marketplace that says, "You will earn money or be paid in proportion to/in exchange for how much value you give yourself and how many people know about it." So you need to be able to shine with your true gifts. Once you feel calm from the first round of Tapping, do a positive round so you can step into a better place for wealth manifestation.

POSITIVE TAPPING SCRIPT
TO SHINE YOUR LIGHT

Say the following phrases aloud while tapping on the karate chop point:

Even though I'm really feeling my vow to stay invisible and it's scary, I took this vow for a reason. I totally honor how I feel about it.

(continued)

Even though this whole idea is triggering me, I have a lot of beliefs around this. I learned them from my family. I'm just going to honor that I am unique. I am one of a kind and I am really good at what I do.

Even though this still feels scary and I still feel vulnerable, I do love bringing my gifts to the world. I put my heart and soul into what I do and I really love sharing that. I'm just going honor that, too.

Now Tap through the points, using the following phrases or your own:

I actually love the way I am *** My training, my intelligence, my unique gifts *** That special quality that I bring to my work *** The world really does need it *** I've spent a lot of time downplaying it *** Hiding it *** Being invisible *** I've spent a lot of time trying to be someone else *** I'm just going to honor that *** But I totally honor how special I am *** How much I love talking about my work.

I pour my heart and soul into it *** And I would really love to share that with more people *** So many more people *** And I totally deserve to receive *** To receive based on my giving *** Based on my amazing value *** I choose to stand here and shine with my unique brilliance *** With my heart open for all to see *** I totally honor that I am a miracle *** I am a rock star *** And I give everyone else permission to shine, too *** Shine fully with their light *** Because I choose to shine fully with my light.

As I shine my brilliance *** The whole universe responds *** And from my actions *** I will receive the exact value back in money and wealth *** In praise and support *** In everything I desire *** I start to let go of my vow to be invisible.

Take a nice deep breath. It's interesting to look at that picture of you in front of a large group again and see how you look now after you said some of those positives for yourself. Often people say, "Wow, I look like I'm shining—like I'm surrounded with white light. It looks like the people are happy, and they all feel empowered." This may be the first time you've felt this power to let the world know how terrific you are from a place of personal honor and truth, not arrogance. The truth is, when you shine with all your brilliance and honor your value, you give permission to everyone around you to do the same. This is profound and will affect everyone you come into contact with for the better. It's inspiring, motivating, and captivating. And you can be that person!

Do Tapping for the vow to be invisible the next time you have to go into a situation where you're either going to market yourself or ask for a raise, or just let people know in a wonderful, heart-centered way that you believe in the power of you—in your own value and the gifts that you want to share more with the world. Then watch what happens. The more you share from this authentic, empowered place, the more people will take notice and remember you, want to be around you, and see you as a confident leader in your field. Some of them will want to pay you what you're worth and some will want to be part of your mission to reach your goals. From this place you enlist fans, supporters, believers, and investors!

You can also use this Tapping to raise your energy and blast through inertia and procrastination. To accomplish your big goal, you'll have to push outside your comfort zone. But this process will make that exciting instead of daunting. It's time to start speaking and acting like a person who sets, deserves, goes after, and achieves big goals! And that person does not stay or play small and invisible. He or she wants to be seen realizing big, outrageous goals!

Your Proof That You Are More Powerful Now Than Ever Before: Is this the right time in your life to make a change and create more wealth? A quick excercise will reveal the answer.
www.TappingIntoWealth.com/Video14

15

BECOMING A
GREAT RECEIVER

D o you tend to try to do everything for yourself? Does not being dependent on anyone matter greatly to you? Would you rather work and be responsible for everything—even to the point of failure—than ask for help? At some point in your life, you may have decided that you're on your own, and you took a vow to never depend on anyone. This is a very common vow that can be tough to break because it's often taken out of necessity when you're young and reinforced over and over in adulthood. As you read these next sentences, do any feel true for you? Have you made a vow to:

- Never be vulnerable
- Never have needs you can't take care of yourself
- Never ask for what you'd really like
- Never rely on anyone
- Never let yourself feel your deepest needs

You may be thinking, "*Yes*, I did, and that makes sense to me!" It can make absolute sense to have a vow to not be vulnerable or needy.

Being vulnerable leaves you open to being hurt. Needing things from people leaves you open to being disappointed. You might also equate it with being needy or a victim, and that doesn't sound good. After all, aren't you supposed to protect yourself? Taking care of your own needs can seem safer and assure you that what needs to get done will be done. You won't have to nag someone to help with something or be stuck if someone lets you down. This vow is often viewed as smart—what seems best for you and totally necessary. Not counting on others protects you from being disappointed or feeling betrayed when they don't come through for you.

Blocking Support

While it may seem practical, there's a big downside to this vow that can specifically keep you from having both more money and more ease in your life and career. When you decide you don't need anything from others or "the world," you block yourself from asking and receiving. If you have a vow to never be vulnerable or needy, you instead become guarded and closed. It's almost impossible to receive when you're in this state. The funny thing is that often, people who made this vow say what they really want is to feel more supported by both money and people. They aren't aware that their vow keeps them from satisfying those desires.

When it comes to setting a big wealth goal, there are two sides to the equation. First is the working, or "doing," part. Most people who aren't good at the second part—receiving—are extremely good and comfortable with the first part. But you must also allow yourself to *receive* all the rewards of your hard work in the forms of money, recognition, and life ease. While logically it would seem like this is the part everyone welcomes, it's problematic if you vow to never be needy. This vow conflicts with the ability to receive praise, recognition, compliments, and attention for achievements. Does this sound like you? Have you ever said something like: "I'm not doing it for the credit" or "I don't need the compliments." In essence, it means that you're doing it for the accomplishment itself and not for the reward. If you want more money, you need to do it for both, admit to it, and be ready and willing to receive.

Those who are willing to openly ask for and receive support recognize that achieving huge goals happens faster when you have enlisted assistance and have people to collaborate with. A support system—whether it's an actual team helping you with your goal, or the emotional and mental support of a peer group—will allow you to expand and capitalize on your brilliance to achieve great things. When you know you can't do it alone, you may feel sad, frustrated, or envious of people who have help if you don't know how to have that for yourself. So, how do you see if this vow is played out in your life? Here's an exercise to test that. Take a deep breath and get comfortable.

Exercise: Are You Open to Receive?

Think back to when you were a child. How well did your parents meet your emotional needs? Were they attentive, loving, and affectionate? Did they allow you to need them? Or were they emotionally absent or critical? Picture yourself as a young child and imagine asking your parents for more attention, love, or a hug. Let it play out on the movie screen of your mind. What happens? Are your parents willing and able to meet your needs? If not, how did you react? Can you see where you took the vow to not ask anymore, maybe to never even feel the impulse to ask?

Let any thoughts come up, even if the memories are painful. The more details you remember, the more you can clear.

Often this is where these vows to never ask for your true needs began. Were you comfortable reaching out to give or get love, affection, attention, and nurturing? Or did you suppress those needs because you learned early that your parents and others were not able or willing to meet them? Some people only remember believing it was fruitless to ask, so they decided to never want anything from their parents, in effect dismissing them as caregivers and going it alone.

If your parents or caregivers didn't have the ability, desire, or capacity to give you what you really needed, that could shut down the very impulse of wanting them. Instead, you might short-circuit feeling your real needs and desires. In effect, you learn to run your true feelings and needs through your thought process of deciding which are appropriate, likely to be met, and not "too needy." Any that don't fit that mold get pushed aside.

Likewise, vowing to never be vulnerable and express your feelings and deepest needs can seem like a good way to protect yourself from further pain and disappointment. These vows are made because you believe they'll keep you strong and safe. They say "no" to needing anything from other people. This fuels determination to take care of yourself. "I can use my brains, I can use my strength, and I can make stuff happen on my own."

For example, Kathy was an extremely hardworking woman who had accomplished a lot in her career as an administrator in a social service organization. She was tired, burnt out, and often had insomnia worrying about her work responsibilities. After admitting to doing the work of two people following a staff member's departure, she said she desperately wanted to find a man to share her life with—someone she could lean on and take vacations with. This had proven difficult, since Kathy worked so much and had no time to date. Plus, the thought of dating made her feel totally guarded. Her few attempts ended in disaster and she comforted herself by saying, "I never get to use my vacation time anyway. I always end up covering for everyone, so there's no time for me to take off."

Kathy couldn't understand why things had turned out this way and felt a lot of resentment toward her staff, who used every last vacation day each year. Yet with all of her sacrifices, she also didn't advance in ways that were commensurate with the work she put in. She was particularly triggered by one woman in her office, who often played the role of a damsel in distress but was able to get raises and promotions because she always asked for them. In addition, Kathy scornfully noted that her co-worker was always being rescued and taken care of by her husband. I pointed out how much judgment and criticism she directed at someone who had exactly what she said she wanted most!

We Tapped on Kathy's judgment and frustration about never being able to allow herself to ask and receive in this way. She revealed that her parents were extremely neglectful, leaving her home alone from a young age, often with no food in the house. From the age of five, she remembers knowing she was on her own, that no one was going to be there for her, and that she had to "suck it up and soldier on." As we Tapped about this, immense sadness came up as she cried for all her unmet needs and how strong and guarded she had to be at such a young age. As Kathy came through the Tapping, she did a lot of self-healing.

She began to honor her needs with baby steps each day by doing small things to care for herself in the way she wanted to be treated. She started taking her long overdue vacation time and hired an additional person so her workload was cut in half. She joked, "I've become quite the slacker and am reveling in it!" Kathy's life changed dramatically as she started to allow herself to feel what she wanted and gave herself permission to enjoy it. Within six months, her new attitude had attracted a new man in her life who loved taking care of her. And new opportunities opened for her at work.

Sometimes these vows can be motivated by lessons taught at home. Parents may teach their sons that they need to take care of themselves, and when they get older, the women in their lives too. Asking for help may be perceived as weak, whereas working hard and soldiering through struggle is perceived as strong. If you want to live up to being self-sufficient—"being a man"—you live through the vow to do everything yourself. Many women were taught to please others and not worry about themselves and their needs because "It's better to give than to receive," which also indirectly instills this vow. No matter what the reasons are for taking it, the vow to not depend on anyone keeps you from receiving all the rewards in life that you want and deserve, including wealth, despite how much you think you want it on a conscious level.

Do the exercise above and really think about your memories to help determine if you took this vow to never ask and never feel your deepest needs—at any time in your life, on any level, however small. Often when I discuss this with clients or attendees at my workshops, the word "depression" comes up, which is logical. Apart from the use of the word "depression" as a clinical diagnosis, you may also depress your deepest feelings, including anger, sadness, passion, and enthusiasm for life.

Now be honest. Did you learn to depress some of your natural feelings and desires? Remember, you never depress the acceptable ones, like the desire to learn, achieve, and excel personally. It's the ones you judge as the most selfish, unacceptable, and embarrassing, or those that lead to vulnerability that get repressed. When you free them, you free yourself to improve not only your financial picture, but also the amount of reward and pleasure in your life and relationships.

ALLOWING YOURSELF TO ASK FOR MORE

"Why don't I have more money?" Being hesitant or refusing to ask for what you want makes it hard to get it. Start by asking for what you want—what you really want. From a Law of Attraction perspective, when you don't allow yourself to have needs, you tell the universe, "I don't need anything from anyone. I don't need rewards for all that I do. I'm willing to work hard and be strong, and give and give and give, and work and work and work. But I'm not comfortable receiving anything for it." In order to receive, you have to be open to it. You have to be willing to ask. That's why it's taught that asking for what you want is the first step for using the Law of Attraction effectively. If there's even the slightest tendency for this kind of vow to keep you from getting all your needs met, it's important to clear it out.

Now we'll do some Tapping about the picture you see from your past that might have created the vow to not depend on anyone. I'll use some of the more common words and feelings that people share with me in the Tapping rounds. Tap along and substitute words that apply to you more. This is a very, very important picture to recognize and a very difficult vow to acknowledge and break because it's taken for reasons that were often meant to keep you safe. Those reasons can continue to sound very smart to your analytical mind, so be prepared for some inner resistance to letting go of this specific vow.

TAPPING SCRIPT FOR THE VOW TO NOT DEPEND ON ANYONE

Say the following phrases aloud while Tapping through all the points:

There I am *** I see it all *** I made a vow to be strong *** To not ask *** To not even feel how much energy I had *** How much desire I had *** How much I wanted love *** To be treasured *** To be seen *** I wanted that at some point, but I had to shut it down.

It wasn't safe *** It was dangerous *** There was pain *** There was criticism *** So I learned to not feel my deepest needs *** My

real wants *** I actually refused and instead I did something else ***
I used my brains *** I used my strength *** I used my loving nature *** And I gave and I gave, and I did and I did *** There was no
receiving coming my way *** So I learned not to ask *** The reality was that asking brings more pain.

Asking brings danger *** Asking brings disappointment *** All
the sadness about this picture *** All the anger about this picture ***
I so wanted to be seen *** I so wanted to be loved *** They never
gave me that *** They couldn't give it to me the way I wanted it ***
So I learned not to ask *** And I haven't been a good receiver since.

Take a nice deep breath and look at that picture again. If this round
hit you hard and triggered a lot of emotion or sadness, keep Tapping
on it until it feels less intense so you can process it. It's incredibly
important to clear the emotions and beliefs from this vow, because it
determines whether or not you'll be willing to receive all sorts of loving, nurturing rewards from the universe, including money and wealth.
Once you've Tapped a few times, that picture should be a bit calmer.
You may have had some "aha" moments as you looked at the picture
and did the Tapping, which gives you more to Tap on. Look at it again
and recognize yourself there as a young child. Answer:

- What were your deepest needs back then? What did you really
  want?
- What has it cost you to shut your early desires down?
- While it was probably a coping mechanism that seemed necessary for survival, to protect you or help you achieve on your
  own, what was the cost to your spirit, your dreams?
- How has your ability to earn more money been affected by
  having to shut down those deepest needs, those deepest desires, and the openness to receive?

What if you could let all of that go and just ask the universe for what you really want, just for the selfish pleasure of having it? Would you love to experience the pleasure of money, the sensory, sensual pleasure and joys in life that money brings? What about in terms of ease, time off, less responsibility? What if it was okay to ask for and receive that? Your energy has to be open to receiving the money you desire. You may have worked hard for years without seeing a change in your finances. If you don't ask, you're not likely to receive. It's time to say, "*Yes, I love reward! I want reward!* I want to feel nurtured and loved and adored by other people in the universe, and to receive wealth and anything else I desire. I can *ask* for it!"

Once you clear out those old vows to take care of everything yourself, money can flow to you more easily since you have more resources and support available. To add more fuel, we'll do a positive round of Tapping to help you change the course that the vow took you in and allow yourself to be open to asking for and receiving a lot more. This is where you ask for and receive what you want, instead of asking for more things to try to achieve or more things to prove or to battle with.

POSITIVE TAPPING SCRIPT TO
OPEN TO RECEIVING

Tap on your list of feelings/thoughts from saying, "My income is not enough." Say the following phrases aloud while tapping on the karate chop point:

Even though I made this vow that made a lot of sense at the time to never ask, never be vulnerable—I never even feel my deepest desires—I'm just going to honor it now. I see the conflict it's causing, because the big thing missing in my life is more receiving—

more pleasure, more joy. I want all the pleasure and joy that money can buy.

Even though I took this vow and I never would have imagined it's connected to money, I totally honor all the ways it's blocked me from receiving—receiving the manifestation of the reward, the pleasure, the nurturing that money represents as an energy, that money can physically purchase. I'm open to letting go of this old vow and taking some baby steps into asking and receiving.

Continue Tapping through all the points, using the following phrases:

But I made a vow to never be vulnerable *** I'm not sure I can let that go *** I never complain about my needs and my feelings *** I'm proud of that *** I'm not sure I can let that go *** But I'm just going to be open to a baby step *** A baby step toward asking *** Opening up to receive all the joys and pleasures *** All the reward I say I want *** I actually love receiving *** I love earning big money *** I enjoy watching it pile up *** And it's so pleasurable to spend *** Spend on me without guilt for the pleasure and enjoyment of it.

I'm open to taking a big step up in honoring my power *** The power that goes beyond vulnerability *** The power to ask for and receive everything I'm wanting to manifest *** I'm actually really powerful *** Do I still need to worry about being vulnerable? *** I will always be an achiever, but what if I could receive and enjoy the reward? *** I'm open to healing this vow *** And allowing a whole new level of receiving into my life.

Now take a deep breath and just see how that round felt as those positive words came out. It can take some time for your subconscious to process this, to have more moments of consciousness about it, and to Tap through it to the point where you feel neutral about the old vow.

It's one of the toughest ones to let go of because you've amassed a million pieces of evidence that prove why that vow to never ask, never be vulnerable, and never acknowledge your feelings makes perfect sense, and this reality seems like the absolute truth. It takes time to rewire how you think and operate to become open to this idea. That's why in the last Tapping round I talked about taking baby steps as you open up to receiving.

You may have to Tap through the rounds in this chapter many times before that old vow is cleared completely. But once it is, you'll be open to receiving a lot more, with a lot less effort in many cases. Keep this in mind as you work through it and become conscious of when you say:

- "I'll take care of it myself."
- "I can do it all myself."
- "That's okay; I'm strong."
- "I don't need much."

Every time you say something like that, you close yourself off from receiving. Remember, you still get to be strong and independent and self-reliant, but you can *also* have your needs met. You can sometimes rely on trustworthy people, so your work is reduced and so you can relax more and maybe even break down and let someone else be strong for you. You can be both self-reliant and supported! So take another nice deep breath and just honor what it's like to ask and receive, and try that out in your life. Open yourself up to one small thing at a time. You might get some surprised looks from friends and family, but it will feel great, especially when your wealth begins to grow!

The Truth About What You Really Want and How to Ask for It: A quick look at your inner child will change forever what you ask for and how you ask. www.TappingIntoWealth.com/Video15

16

I *Refuse* to Be Rich!

W hy would anyone refuse to be rich? Consciously, you probably believe you'd *love* to be rich! Think about suddenly earning double or triple your current income, or making millions. Wouldn't that be great? Not according to your subconscious mind! Throughout the book, I've discussed a multitude of reasons why your subconscious mind refuses to let you become wealthy or advance significantly beyond your current wealth set point. Until you clear them all, your subconscious will refuse to allow you to reach your high goals for income and success. This chapter reminds you of some blocks that might still be sticking around and helps you look for any remaining messages that subconsciously say, "I refuse to be rich." Once you clear them, you'll be in a good place to change your financial picture for the better.

Negative Messages about Being Rich

Your subconscious is almost 85 percent of your mind, and its primary purpose is to keep you safe; therefore, if it interprets being rich as unsafe, it will use all of its powers to "protect" you. If your subconscious mind believes it's dangerous to be wealthy, it will keep you poor, regardless of your income, your true value, or even your belief in your value. The exercises below will reveal how this may operate for you in a very personal way. Why would your subconscious mind believe it's not safe to be rich? Often it's filled with experiences and programs that conclude it's not. As discussed in chapter 5, early programming from your parents and family may fill you with messages about the evils of greed and money and the corruption and sinning of the rich. For example:

- "The rich are arrogant, dishonest, and don't care about people."
- "Money corrupts even good people."
- "Rich people think they're better than you and have problems you wouldn't want."

Did your early religious training set a tone for how you view having lots of money? In some religions, there are messages that the rich are greedy, worship money, will kill or cheat for it, and will never get into heaven. In fact, many religious figures first gave away all their riches and lived as paupers to attain a higher level of spirituality. Catholic nuns and priests take a vow of poverty to serve God. Of course it's not healthy to worship money and use people, but programming can give you beliefs that tend to be extreme. I've heard:

- "You can't be rich and spiritual."
- "Money is a false idol. The rich worship money."
- "Better to be happy than rich!"

TV shows and movies often depict rich people—the bosses or business owners—as villains focused on using people for money. They seem idiotic, self-centered, or odious. Rich characters in films hurt people to get what they want, ignoring their families or stepping on hardworking, honest people as they climb to the top. And we, the audience, enthusiastically root for their downfall and cheer when it comes. Some older TV shows in particular portrayed those with money or power as bumbling idiots or as aloof, arrogant, snobby, entitled, selfish, and materialistic. An example from my childhood is the Howells, the older couple on *Gilligan's Island*, who were comical because they were as selfish, entitled, and self-important as they were completely clueless and idiotic.

You may not think about these associations consciously, but they come up when you see media coverage of rich people ripping off those with much less income or committing a crime—adding to their negative image. The negativity increases if the person gets away with it, as when corrupt executives get caught but still live in the lap of luxury, or "get fired" with multimillion-dollar bonuses or severance packages. Or you see Donald Trump or Paris Hilton types spend ridiculous amounts of money on large excesses, like gold toilets or diamond jewelry for their dogs, while you can't afford even a cheap car or a vacation.

Your subconscious mind records all this, along with your parents' negative beliefs about being rich. As far-fetched as it may seem, your mind makes a connection between your becoming wealthy and great emotional pain and loss. You may believe that if you get rich, your friends and family will treat you very differently or be suspicious, jealous, uncomfortable, or nasty. They may even seem to wish for your downfall. The subconscious mind can find many reasons for why you should *never* become rich. Your most deeply wired and primitive survival instinct may believe you're safer and will survive better if you refuse wealth. This needs to be rewired if you want to successfully create a new wealth reality. This kind of programming even overrides consciously knowing there are philanthropists and other wealthy people who do lots of good.

Many people recall money causing problems in their family—

arguing, worry, stress over how it should be saved or spent. Think about the paradigm work you did in chapter 5. As a child, were you caught in battles around money? Or maybe you had a bit more than friends growing up and felt different or guilty about it. The messages in your subconscious may be loud and clear:

Money = Anger/Conflict/Guilt

When money brings up memories of conflict, you'll find ways to avoid or get rid of it. Another side of this is if a parent used money (or what it can buy) to make up for what they couldn't give in time, attention, or affection. If you experienced money equaling love, a host of strange habits and reactions around money and overspending can be triggered.

THE MONEY SHADOW #1

If you want to substantially increase your wealth, it's critically important to clear any lingering negative associations with being wealthy, and to free yourself from unconscious habits that sabotage your wealth and savings goals, even if you don't think these issues relate to you. If you believe you love rich people and can't wait to be rich, try the exercises anyway. Often clients who don't believe this would apply to them are amazed by the programming they find by doing one.

To find your programming and get a baseline for its emotional intensity, do two exercises using what I call the "money shadow." This is the dark side to money and people who have it. The money shadow reflects all your negative beliefs about being wealthy and all the actions, attitudes, and focus you think are required to amass wealth. In this first exercise, you'll step into the shoes of the money shadow to see how your subconscious resistance to wealth drives you to survive and avoid pain by staying within your tribe's beliefs.

Exercise for Money Shadow #1

Revisit the visualization you did in chapter 5 on your earliest money paradigm. Take a nice deep breath, close your eyes, and bring up that picture of you at maybe six or seven. Your parents or caregivers are talking about how they feel about money and wealth. The picture should be calmer, since you did a lot of Tapping on it already.

Now, imagine stepping into this picture as an adult with your childhood parents after achieving your goals for both income and work hours. You're dressed in expensive clothing, with a shopping bag full of more, and feeling relaxed and healthy from a massage. You've dropped in to tell your parents-of-the-past how much you make—several times more than they did—and how many hours you work to earn that much. You also share how much money you saved. Then share that you're about to jump into a limo with three millionaires for a night on the town, before leaving on a big vacation. Note how you feel, look, act, and anything they say to you.

I doubt you'd announce it to your parents like this, but the exercise will reveal your deepest programmed resistance to being wealthy and force you to break your vows of loyalty to fitting in with your tribe, specifically in terms of their views on wealth, so you can see the perceived downside. It forces you to become the "money shadow" so you can see how black and white your programming is. I've done this exercise with thousands of people, and it's amazing how painful, negative, and uncomfortable the picture becomes. I often hear:

- "My parents are looking at me like I'm a criminal."
- "They're judging and disapproving of me."
- "They suspect I'm doing something wrong/illegal to make that much without working as hard as they did."

- "I feel horrible saying this to them. They look disempowered."
- "My parents are simple people and wouldn't relate to that kind of money."

The emotions can be summed up as feeling like an outcast, judged, or suddenly uncomfortable and different around family. Whether illogical or not, this unconscious, negative perception of becoming wealthy is very painful and never spoken about.

Repeat this exercise while picturing your friends and colleagues to get similar information. The most clearly telling feeling is, "I'd no longer fit in or be comfortable around them, and they'd be uncomfortable around me." The strongest emotions people report are feeling bad, guilty, embarrassed, or ashamed when declaring their income and balanced lifestyle. The other common theme is feeling bad or sorry for their family or friends, or angry at their unsupportive reaction. Also notice what kinds of judgments your parents have specifically about the three millionaires waiting in the car. What would they say about people who've made millions and about the fact that you're going out on the town with them? Be very specific as you write down everything you learn in this exercise.

This exercise worked well for Dr. Ellen, a chiropractic doctor. After twenty-six years of practice, her love for her practice continued to deepen, but her financial rewards weren't aligned with how much she should earn with her combination of great passion and hard work. While she built a successful practice serving thousands of happy patients, she came to me because she had no savings or retirement accounts and earned just enough to pay business and personal expenses. When I asked Dr. Ellen for her feelings about wealthy people, she said she believed there were lots of good, generous, and philanthropic ones. But she remembered that her father had said many times, "Wealth corrupts you!"

She had just had dinner with him and shared how exciting the thought of being a multimillionaire was and how she'd do all these great things with that money. Her father became adamant that this was the worst thing that could happen to her. "It will ruin you, Ellen!" he said over and over. She argued, "But, Dad, this is me speaking. I'd do wonderful things with that money." But he was stubbornly sure this would corrupt her as if it were an absolute fact. She was speechless. Dr. Ellen clearly saw in that moment how some of her negative beliefs about wealth were instilled. She'd grown up in a household that struggled financially, and her reality was a life of inadequate income.

Dr. Ellen realized that she and her siblings got messages every day that there's not enough for everyone. So some people have and others don't. She recognized how uncomfortable she felt from the belief that she had to take more from others in order to do well. She also acknowledged that her financial picture of just getting by as an adult was still an improvement over her childhood financial situation, so she unconsciously settled for that, set small, safe goals, and didn't manage her money well enough to accumulate any wealth. When I pressed her to set a huge goal for her personal income from her practice, she also became aware of what she called "the ultimate money shadow that hangs over many healers"—the idea that somehow it's wrong to become wealthy by helping people get well.

Most wealthy doctors she knew were M.D.s. One drove a $250,000 car in front of his patients and treated them dismissively, writing prescriptions for complaints instead of supporting their healing. Many of Dr. Ellen's patients had similar stories about former caregivers. She didn't want to be associated with the "rich doctors" or have patients see her as profiting from their suffering. She experienced a huge "aha" moment when she recognized the conflict in wanting to be a good doctor who was also wealthy. As we cleared these negative and limiting beliefs and shadows with Tapping, she felt anger and sadness at how much these programmed beliefs cost her. She had spent many promising years just getting by, which limited her and her family's lives.

After our work together, Dr. Ellen profoundly changed how she managed her practice, calling it, "stepping into the CEO shoes," which she had always avoided. Her goals got higher. She began managing money much more consciously and learning how to build a more profitable business. In the next year, her profit grew by 50 percent and she doubled her savings and retirement accounts. The best part was that as she focused on running her business like a savvy CEO, she was able to expand it into a true holistic healing center—her ultimate dream. She attracted talented practitioners and new tenants, including an M.D. who sent her referrals and attended her workshops.

The Tapping below is intended to reduce the intensity of negative emotions, separate your goals for wealth from unconscious fears of being rejected by your tribe, and bring more clarity and consciousness to your goals for a new wealth reality. For the best results, strongly hone in on words that reflect what you visualized and the feelings it gave you.

TAPPING SCRIPT FOR MONEY SHADOW #1

Tap through the points while picturing the scene in the exercise:

There they are (my parents) *** Judging me/suspecting me *** Maybe even suspecting I am doing something wrong *** Or have been corrupted *** It's so uncomfortable *** I feel embarrassed *** Ashamed *** And really awkward.

I have just made everyone upset and uncomfortable *** I feel like

I am being arrogant *** Rude *** Insensitive *** My parents worked so hard *** And I am showing them it's easy for me *** This is very scary *** I feel bad.

Maybe they are even hostile to me/rejecting me *** Or asking me for a handout *** Expecting me to fix everything now *** I feel awful *** I feel bad for them *** Maybe they are trying to be proud *** But I know the truth *** They look at me differently now *** They suspect or judge me.

Everything has changed now *** Because now I am the rich *** I am the wealthy *** I am different from them *** Maybe they even hate or shun me now *** Maybe they feel judged by me *** I really don't like how this feels *** It's embarrassing.

Confrontational *** Disempowering *** Sad *** I never want this to happen!

Now take a look at the picture in your imagination again. It should appear and feel less charged. Continue on to the next round of Tapping to really bring up the awareness of this programming so it loses its power over you.

MORE TAPPING FOR MONEY SHADOW #1

Tap again through the points:

Wow, I am really seeing this programming *** All the ways *** It does not feel safe or good *** To be wealthy *** And how wrong it

(continued)

feels to work *** Less than my parents had to work *** When I look at this *** I realize that I do have resistance.

Really uncomfortable resistance *** To the exact goals I have set *** For my wealth *** And life balance *** This is a big conflict for me *** Even though it seems crazy *** And illogical *** My feelings reveal it all.

I am just going to breath through this *** Honor it *** And know that my awareness and consciousness are powerful *** I am open to releasing *** All this survival programming *** That has connected a no-win situation with my becoming wealthy *** That has connected pain *** Embarrassment *** Conflict *** Rejection *** And judgment from my family and friends *** With me becoming rich *** I am opening to letting the light of consciousness shine on this primitive drive *** To stay safe in my tribe of origin *** My family *** By literally keeping me stuck financially *** So that I can let it go.

I don't need this running! *** I choose to be free *** And loved/welcomed *** And totally safe *** While becoming much more wealthy *** Meeting all my goals *** And working in a way that I love!

You should feel good after that round. This is a great affirmation to use daily, with or without Tapping, and will always raise your consciousness and bring you to a strong sense of presence about your life, your goals, and your choices.

THE MONEY SHADOW #2

In this second exercise, you'll turn the tables and uncover programming you've internalized from your parents, religious upbringing, society, and the media. You'll see limiting beliefs you have about being wealthy by looking at a different angle of the money shadow.

EXERCISE FOR MONEY SHADOW #2

Picture someone who has created a tremendous amount of wealth—someone you have a hard time not judging and don't fully respect, whom you know your parents would judge and complain about. This person represents the money shadow for you.

Next, close your eyes and picture that person like you're looking right at him/her. How does he/she look to you and what's your judgment about him/her? Give yourself permission to be very honest, even nasty. Is she arrogant, selfish, or wasteful? Is he unkind, snobby, or money grubbing? Is she all about money and doesn't care about people? Write down everything you feel very specifically because, believe it or not, it will be directly tied to the gift you'll get at the other side of the next Tapping round.

This is where Tapping is used to voice your righteous judgment about this person, who represents your money shadow. The script uses the most common judgments I hear. Please add your own feelings in place of those that don't apply to you.

TAPPING SCRIPT FOR MONEY SHADOW #2

Tap through the points, just like you're looking at this person:

There they are *** Look at them *** So rich *** So arrogant *** They think they're better than everyone *** They think they're better than me *** And so corrupt *** So selfish.

They don't care about anyone *** Just money *** Totally focused on money *** Selfishly focused on themselves *** Totally material-

(continued)

istic *** I never want to be like that *** I would never be like that ***
And my family and friends would agree with me.

What an awful example of wealth *** I totally judge it *** And
I'm totally right *** Arrogant and selfish *** Really don't care about
the important things *** Like people *** They probably screwed
people *** To get to the top.

Hurt people to get to the top *** I totally judge them *** And I
totally should *** My parents would agree with me *** My friends
would agree with me *** I never want to be anything like that *** I
refuse to be wealthy like that *** I don't want anything to do with
wealth like that.

Take a nice deep breath and notice how freeing it can feel to voice
resistance to that money shadow in a very honest, even over-the-top,
way. Close your eyes and picture that person again. See how he/she looks
to you now. How much do they trigger feelings of dislike in you? What's
the intensity around your judgment toward him/her? Even after just one
round of Tapping, it's usually a lot less. If you still feel a strong negative
judgment, push against this person, Tap through the round again.

THE GIFT OF THE MONEY SHADOW

Now for the part about the money shadow that takes an especially open
mind. Your feelings about it offer you a special gift in that they teach
you about qualities you lack that can assist you in building your wealth,
if you work on developing them. This person may have done unfair or
corrupt things but he/she reflects what you should know about yourself
to improve your life and your financial picture. They may have built
wealth in negative ways and be arrogant and selfish, but a gift is revealed through their shadow when you can look beyond your negative
attitude and see them more objectively.

If you examine some of the main judgments you have about rich people, one at a time, you might start to understand what benefits they get from what you see as their negative qualities. For example, a big judgment I hear about often is the arrogance of rich people. While I don't advocate being arrogant, think about what an arrogant person experiences. The top answers I get are:

- "They experience their own power."
- "They ask for what they want, and get it."
- "They honor their value and are never underpaid."

People often struggle with these issues. If you could adopt a piece of this shadow, give yourself permission to own more of your power, ask for what you want, and honor your value—wouldn't that be a gift for your life? You can do these things without turning into a horrible, arrogant person, but a dab more of the gift of arrogance can transform your net worth! *Often what you judge, hate, and rail against the most is the dark side of something that you actually need more of.* But you can adopt some of the lighter side of these qualities. What does a person who's a little more selfish or self-focused get to experience? The top answers I get are:

- "They're able to set boundaries."
- "They put themselves higher on their priority list."
- "They put a lot more attention, energy, and focus on the wealth creation that makes them feel good, safe, and rich."

People admit these statements reflect their biggest day-to-day challenges—what they avoid doing because it seems selfish. Are you beginning to see what gifts this shadow teaches you? There's also a gift in being materialistic and money-focused. Rich people manage and handle large amounts of money in ways that amass wealth. They make sure to be expert at this and prioritize money management and financial gain. Wouldn't doing some of that be a gift for you? This side of the money shadow helps you start to see that even though this person is negative, the entire feeling behind "I'll never be like that" prevents you from having a higher level of wealth or using healthier versions of qualities you don't like, both of which would help you to own your money power. Learning from these gifts helps you:

- Focus on creating the wealth you really want
- Have the "arrogance" to declare your value and ask for what you want, since people who do that often get it
- Set boundaries that prioritize you and your financial well-being

Tapping on this will bring it all together so you can get to the other side—owning your power around money. The biggest gift in the money shadow work is the clarity and permission to become a really good money manager. Too many people walk around saying, "I'm not good at handling money" because they've often made a vow to never be anything like the money shadow.

TAPPING SCRIPT FOR THE GIFT OF THE MONEY SHADOW

So let's do another round of Tapping, starting on the karate chop point:

Even though I really judge this wealthy person, and I'm right about a lot of that, I'm open to seeing the conflict in this for me. I've been refusing to be anything like that because of the rejection, the disempowerment, and all the judgment it would get me in life. I judge this person. If I were to be wealthy, everyone would judge me that way.

Even though I really judge this money-shadow person, I'm open to seeing the conflict in it. This vow to be nothing like them doesn't let me receive the gift.

This person has some gifts for me; for me personally, a calling to step into my power around money. I'm open to receiving that gift right now. I'm open to stepping into the part of me that is a million-dollar money manager; who would love to handle, earn, amass, and manage millions of dollars.

Now continue Tapping through the points:

I have a lot of judgment *** And so does everyone I know *** I totally understand my push against wealth *** I see now that *** I've managed to get rid of my money *** To avoid ever looking like this person *** I totally honor this push against the money shadow *** All their negative traits are so clear.

And I never really want to be like that *** But I'm open to the gifts in this for me *** The gifts in arrogance *** A beautiful little gift in a negative word like "arrogance" *** A tiny bit more arrogance in my life might serve me *** I'm open to the gift in being selfish *** A tiny little gift in such a bad word *** Being a little more selfish around my life, my wealth, my goals.

That would be a gift for me *** I'm open to the gift in being focused on money *** Too much focus is not in balance *** But too little focus is causing me to be poor *** I'm open to the gift in being focused on money *** Focused in a way *** That lets me bring my brilliance *** My intelligence *** My energy *** To all my dealings with money.

I'm open to growing myself *** Into a million-dollar money man-

(continued)

ager *** Earning *** Handling *** Managing very large amounts of money *** And being the wealthy person that is congruent *** Loving *** Compassionate *** And much more generous *** Than I can be now.

I'm totally open to growing myself *** Into a really good money manager *** I may not be that person today *** But I commit to growing myself *** As I do this.

I let the universe know *** It can send me a lot of money *** I can handle it *** I can manage it *** I will do right by that money *** I totally honor my innate brilliance *** And I'm now allowing that focus *** To include money and wealth amassment for my highest good.

Take a nice deep breath. The second exercise of the money shadow work is a bit different, because it's hard to see a gift in the millionaire you pictured in a very negative light. But I hope you enjoyed Tapping for the money shadow, and allowing this process to call you into your power around money in a bigger, richer, and fuller way. Imagine if you put even 20 percent of your energy, focus, and intelligence on your income and savings goals. If you stop allowing your subconscious to refuse to be rich, you can start to imagine all of the ways that you could amass money to build more security and wealth in your life. Say *yes* to that and begin!

Transforming Your Wealth Identity: How someone you admire can help you define who you are becoming
www.TappingIntoWealth.com/Video16

17

THE FIVE DISCIPLINES
FOR CREATING A NEW
VIBRATION ABOUT MONEY

W hy don't I have more money?" Having read the book, I
hope you now have many clues and insights to consider.
The programming and paradigms of the past are as in-
sidious as they are powerful because they operate below your level of
consciousness. But as you use the exercises to shine a light of consciousness on your unconscious patterns and use Tapping to clear them, you
give yourself the opportunity to become free.

Getting to that freedom starts with the "aha" moment from the insight and clarity to see your patterns and how they're connected to your
present reality and daily actions. The work continues into the mind/
body connection by using Tapping to release energy charges—the emotions and limiting beliefs from the patterns. As that weight lifts, you'll
begin to have a new clarity and perspective of openness and possibility
that will help you start making new choices. A lot has been covered,
much of it from the ground up, to reach this point. But to truly create
an entirely new level of wealth, there are five keys I recommend you
adopt. These are disciplines that will help you reach your goals if you
commit to them as a daily practice.

Five Keys for Reaching Goals

First, make a commitment to regularly observe and "catch yourself in the act" of falling into old patterns that limit what you can have or do, or any tendency to go into battle with yourself, others, or your efforts to be successful. If you become consciously aware of your old habits that are related to how you think and respond to money, as well as potential opportunities to make more, you'll be able to take charge, instead of letting old programs and paradigms control you. Each time you catch these patterns operating in your present, find the strength within yourself to challenge them—right then and there. Use my exercises and the Tapping as needed, and you'll break through these tendencies in the quickest fashion.

Second, commit to showing up more fully engaged and charged up everyday! Make an effort to catch yourself anytime you're not "all in" or you're just going through the motions, and stop right there and get re-engaged. Look at your goal and ask yourself, "How badly do I want it?" If the answer is "A *lot*!" take a moment to bring your energy up. You can generate more energy, passion, and desire from within if you want it badly enough. Jump up and down and shout "I want it!" if necessary. When you become more present, more energized, and more fully engaged, everything you do and say will have added impact and power. From that vibe will come resources, clients, partners, and money that will line up for you. Enthusiasm, excitement, and passion are qualities that can take you far beyond someone who has none, even if they have brains, ideas, and resources.

Third, commit to taking action and doing everything needed to get the action going. This means you should give yourself time to dream and brainstorm, allowing ideas to come and inspire you. It also involves figuring out some first steps and making a plan to implement them. Put them on your calendar. Pencil in the action needed and create self-imposed deadlines to mark your progress. Even better, get an account-ability partner with whom you speak for at least fifteen minutes a week to review your goals and action plans and to commit to a timeline. You can work together to encourage each other to reach your goals. You'll also feel less alone in your journey to a much higher level of wealth by having someone on your side.

Your efficiency and effectiveness will thrive in a climate of positive, freely chosen accountability. Many people resist commitment and ac-countability because it can feel a bit like reporting to another boss. But if you want to reach your goals badly enough, you'll get there expon-entially faster if you hold yourself accountable to your own plans. You can decide by asking yourself, "How *soon* do I want it?" If the answer is "Very soon!" choose accountability strategies that will keep you focused and resolute about getting the necessary steps done. You're less likely to let old patterns control you if you have to report your progress to someone. Eventually, as you feel more comfortable operating in the new paradigm you're creating, you might be less likely to need someone watching your progress to make sure you don't backslide. But for now, work with someone if possible.

Fourth, take a minute to review all your plans and goals. Then do something that may seem counterintuitive: give yourself full permis-sion to choose *not* to accomplish your goals and to forget the whole thing. Yes, I'm advising that you acknowledge that it's okay to quit your goals! Give yourself permission to just walk away and keep your life and money exactly the same as today, and enjoy what you have now. This suggestion may surprise you, but it's an important step, so don't take it lightly. The truth is, you don't have to choose to work on your goal; you don't have to commit; you don't have to do another new or different thing. Honor that, because you must give yourself permission to walk away and not choose your goal. The moment you tell yourself "you have to do it," you lose power and become a slave to your goal. True choice is knowing you don't have to do something and choosing it anyway. Then it's truly *your* preference if you consciously decide to go for it.

If you don't consciously choose your goal of a new wealth reality, it will become just another obligation that you think you have to do, that you must do, that makes sense to do. It will eventually feel like work, an imposition or something to rebel against. In order to make it a real choice, there must be options to choose from. That's why it's important to acknowledge that you have the choice of not going after this goal. Feeling you have only one option isn't a choice and can put pressure on you. Knowing it's okay to stay where you are feels much better, since you know you don't have to pursue the goal if it doesn't feel right. Yet having choices makes it more comfortable to choose the path to more wealth.

I want you to have full permission to not choose it and walk around holding on to that choice. Can you feel the lightness and freedom of having that permission? When you choose something as big as the new wealth goal you set, you need to be fully free to do so and fully conscious of what your choice means. If you've given yourself a choice, and after considering all the options, decide to truly, freely, and consciously choose your goal, then your new work will begin and continue. Tomorrow, when you awake, you must look at your goal again, along with the plans, strategies, and actions you're taking and planning, and choose it fully again. You must completely and honestly review, decide, and re-choose your goal every day. When you do that, you truly become empowered and can count yourself as part of a small percentage of people who operate at that level of conscious choice in their lives.

There is, however, one downside because there's something you have to give up when you make a truly conscious choice—complaining! You must accept everything that comes with your choice. You are choosing the extra work, new self-discipline, sacrifices, and so on that come with it. That means you no longer get to complain about them. When you choose consciously, you also take total responsibility for your choices in every moment, even the difficult ones. Having the extraordinary freedom of conscious decision making about what you want to create comes at the price of taking radical responsibility for those choices. The more you make this your practice, the more you'll look around and see that complaining is only the luxury of the disempowered. Owning your choices means also owning all that comes with them.

This doesn't mean that you won't have hard, challenging, and unexpected things appear that you'd like to complain about. Stuff will happen that triggers frustration, disappointment, and stress. The difference is in how you handle it. Get in touch with what you really feel in those difficult moments and honor what gets triggered in you. Don't deny it. Yet in the midst of that dark place, you must steadfastly know that you are *still* choosing every bit of it. Why are you still choosing it? The answer is always the same: "Because I really do want my goal!" This is why a new level of self-discipline, energy, and true desire for your goal must be found within you and cultivated daily. It's one thing to have a moment of excitement and set a huge goal, and another to go the distance, taking action consistently and enthusiastically.

This brings me to my **fifth** key. Trust and shine both your light and your dark. There will be moments of fear, anger, and loss of faith because you're human and don't achieve or evolve beyond your humanity. You evolve into your greatness through your humanity. Accept that within you there's an impulse for:

- Fear *and* courage
- Greed *and* generosity
- Laziness *and* achievement
- Stupidity *and* brilliance

You'll always have both. As you own this fact, walk around with that knowledge and accept who you are anyway. That's when you become unstoppable! When you deeply know this truth about yourself—

"Yes, sometimes I can be a real idiot but I'm also incredibly brilliant"—you free yourself from the exhausting work of hiding your flaws. When you can admit to yourself and others, "I really am afraid of being judged, a total chicken sometimes, *but* I am also brave, courageous, and sometimes a hero," you'll feel a soaring sense of lightness and invincibility.

Becoming Imperfectly Successful

When you set a very big goal, it will push you far beyond your comfort zone. This will trigger many emotions in you. But now you have an incredible tool in being able to use Tapping to reduce fear and self-judgment, while you still own that you're human. Know that you'll be afraid at times, worry about failure, be scared of judgment, and be overly hard on yourself. It comes with being human. During those times, remember that you also have it in you to be fearless, invincible, unstoppable, and focused. You can have this huge goal, create a new wealth reality, *and* still get to be the real, flawed, amazingly imperfect, yet perfect *you*. So be you and choose to be *great*—the bigger, bolder, more real, on fire, and *alive* you. When you do that, this goal will become so much more! It will facilitate both a fabulous new level of wealth in your life and an incredible journey of becoming more authentically you.

Here is some final Tapping that will reflect these keys and put you into a good frame of mind to go forward in pursuing your money goals:

TAPPING SCRIPT FOR BECOMING SUCCESSFUL

Tap through all the points, using the following phrases:

I have this huge, outrageous goal *** I'm asking a lot of myself in this *** In the growth I've had so far *** I've learned so much about me *** And I am ready to move forward *** But I'm just going to honor myself for a minute *** Where I am right now.

I'm human *** So at some level I'm stuck *** I'm overwhelmed *** I'm terrified *** I'm a chicken *** I'm insecure *** I'm disillusioned *** I'm angry at the world *** And I'm sad *** I'm all those things because I'm human *** And I also am amazing *** Really smart *** I have a really big heart *** And I do have big dreams *** I have a big goal for my wealth *** And dreams, and visions about where I want to go *** Some are fleeting and some I really want! *** And this big goal *** I really do want it *** I totally honor that too.

In this present moment *** I am both a mess and a miracle *** I am both my old stories *** And my power *** I am everything I have been *** And I am standing on the precipice of everything I will be *** It's kind of awesome *** It's a big responsibility *** Everyone else I see is going through life sleepwalking *** But now I'm aware of all of this *** It's awesome *** And an awesome responsibility *** I have so much freedom of choice that it's scary *** It's hard to leave sleepwalking.

I honor who I am right now *** With all my fears *** All my limiting beliefs *** And all my vision *** All my dreams *** All my heart's desires and my mission *** I honor all of me *** And I'm open to moving forward *** Toward outrageous healing *** Outrageous choice *** Outrageous goals *** And I'm going to need some support along the way.

(continued)

This is hard and I'm doing it *** So I'm asking for support back *** From the entire universe *** The divine *** I would like some inspiration *** I would like some confirmation *** That would be really nice *** I would love some divine direction *** I would love amazing people to show up to help me *** I would like gold to arise in my life *** In any form that's right for me *** Inspiration, ideas, coincidences *** Or miracles *** Or amazing people *** I'm open and allowing everything I need *** To show up *** To both support my humanity *** And further my vision *** To help me heal *** Help me step up *** Help me have courage *** And help me create everything I am envisioning *** I'm open to expecting and anticipating that help.

And I am willing to do my part *** I will commit and take action *** Like never before *** I will catch myself in the act *** Of limiting myself *** Sabotaging myself *** Or playing small *** And I will bring my energy up and remember *I want it!* *** I will remember it's possible for me *** Because I am a creator *** My eyes are opening wider *** I am seeing things I have never noticed before *** So much abundance and possibility *** And I'm seeing so much more in me *** And I am asking for more from me *** The courage *** The brilliance *** The enthusiasm *** The words *** The vision for my outrageous goal.

I hope that this book has helped you move closer to the wealth you'd love and deserve to have. I know how it feels to be introduced to a new technique that triggers uncomfortable memories and also seems ridiculous at first. After all, my background is engineering. But, boy, am I glad I gave it a chance! It does seem like a strange technique for doing such a big job. If you've spent years trying to get out of your money rut, Tapping points on your face and body may seem way too simplistic to be able to make a difference. But it does!

Having gone through the same doubts, skepticism, and fear as you,

I can attest that it works. I wouldn't have my career, had I not been open-minded enough to try what sounded like a silly technique—Tapping. I sincerely hope that you've been able to use this mighty tool to find your own new wealth reality. Always remember that you have it in you to be very rich—in dollars and cents! So go for it and enjoy the money it brings. You *deserve* to have more money—lots more! And the power to get there is all in your mind and your fingertips.

Creating a Life of Wealth, Meaning, and Impact:
Final words about following your heart with courage
and faith
www.TappingIntoWealth.com/Video17

ACKNOWLEDGMENTS

Acknowledgments from Margaret M. Lynch

I want to thank Alan Davidson, my friend and a true king among men . . . what would I do without you? Your friendship and direction has been a guiding light to my mission and happiness!

To Nick, Jessica, and Alex Ortner, thank you for giving me a chance to shine all those years ago and supporting me in the most amazing and miraculous ways!

To my amazingly beautiful and powerful daughter, Emma: your birth changed my life forever . . . and me forever. You inspire me every day, make me laugh every day, and I love you . . . every day!

I want to say a very special thanks to my parents Peter and Marguerite, who went on a mission to raise eight empowered, educated, and totally loved children . . . and were successful. Thank you for believing in me and encouraging me every second of this "off the corporate path" career. Thank you to my seven brothers and sisters and all their spouses for being the most amazing and supportive family on the planet.

To my lifelong best friend and "Irish twin" Annie: I am truly grateful for having you in my life ever-knowing we will always be there for each other . . . like, ALWAYS. I thank you for bringing me the beautiful gifts that are Katie and Hope (along with Mack, Oliver, and SmoJoe) whom I treasure and miss even five minutes after you leave.

To Bethaney, my partner in all things coaching and Saturday teas that go on for twelve hours. I love my job because I get to "go to work" with you! Thank you for your amazing friendship, brilliance, AND zany sense of humor! You GET me, and I get you!

To my indomitable tribe of pals—Karen, Sherry, Peggy—how I adore having you in my life and always look forward to our hysterical outings. Together with my oldest and dearest friends Whendy, Melissa, and Jessica, you have all been my rock of support, connection, and caring, often going above and beyond in "listening to me ramble on" sessions that I truly needed.

I want to thank Rhys Thomas for your genius in explaining how the chakra vows work and allowing me to discuss them in this book.

Thank you to Suze Orman for being the first person to ask me to examine my beliefs about money and start me on a path of awakening in all areas of my life. Thank you to David Bach and Loral Langemeier for teaching me how to pay myself first, and to Wayne Dyer for inspiring me to leave the corporate world and follow my inner voice to the great unknown.

Special appreciation goes to the smartest women on the planet—Pamela Bruner, Suzanne Evans, and Lisa Sasevich—for teaching me how to build a real business.

And a special thank-you to Daylle Deanna Schwartz for believing in me and turning my teachings into a fabulous book!

Acknowledgments from Daylle Deanna Schwartz

First I'd like to thank God and the universe for all my blessings. Great BIG thanks to Margaret M. Lynch for the total pleasure of working on this book with her and for the improvement in my life from the lessons in it. A VERY special thank-you to intuition teacher and founder of PoweredbyIntuition .com, Angela Artemis, who heard me speaking about a problem I was struggling with and generously offered to teach me a crazy new energy technique called EFT/Tapping, which changed my life. It led me to learn how to use it better for myself and my counseling clients, which led me to Margaret.

If you enjoyed this book, visit

www.tarcherbooks.com

and sign up for Tarcher's e-newsletter to receive
special offers, giveaway promotions, and
information on hot upcoming releases.

TARCHER
PENGUIN

Great Lives Begin with Great Ideas

Connect with the Tarcher Community

. . .

Stay in touch with favorite authors!
Enter weekly contests!
Read exclusive excerpts!
Voice your opinions!

Follow us

 Tarcher Books

 @TarcherBooks

If you would like to place a bulk order
of this book, call 1-800-847-5515.

This updated and expanded edition of the alternative-health
classic shows readers how they can understand their
body's energy systems to promote healing.
978-1-58542-650-8 $17.99

DONNA EDEN
Bestselling author of Energy Medicine and Energy Medicine for Women
WITH DONDI DAHLIN

Includes the
Five-Minute
Daily Energy
Medicine
Routine

THE LITTLE BOOK OF
ENERGY MEDICINE
The Essential Guide to
Balancing Your Body's Energies

The Little Book of Energy Medicine is a simple, easy-to-use "pocket guide"
to one of the most powerful alternative health practices in existence
today, from world-renowned healer Donna Eden.

978-1-58542-931-8

$14.95

The ultimate edition of the all-time prosperity bestseller!
Think and Grow Rich by Napoleon Hill has become the must-have bible
of prosperity and success for millions of readers since its initial publication in
1937. Now from the number one publisher of Napoleon Hill's books comes
the most complete and essential edition of *Think and Grow Rich* yet.

978-1-58542-896-0

$18.95